SCALE COLOUR SYSTEM
VISUALISE THE FRETBOARD &
UNLOCK YOUR PLAYING

Alex Lofoco

*An **intuitive method** for learning
all the notes on the fretboard.*

BASS

Vol. 1 – Scales

*Map and internalise Notes, Scales and Shapes
over the entire fretboard to **develop accuracy**
and **unlock your playing**.*

Book design and illustrations by Alex Lofoco.
Proofreader Lorenzo Milani.

ISBN 978-1-9999047-9-1

www.alexlofoco.com

Contents

HEPTATONIC SCALES

SYMMETRICAL SCALES

R = Root – starting note
S = Semitone (Half Step) – one fret space
T = Tone (Whole Step) – two fret space

FRETTING HAND

F.H. = Fretting Hand
1Fpf = One Finger per fret spacing
5fpS = Five frets per String (stretched position)

Fretting Hand digit

1 = index finger
2 = middle finger
3 = ring finger
4 = pinky

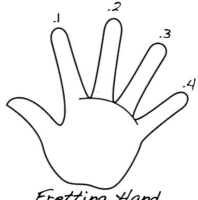

Fretting Hand

1NpS = One Note per String
2NpS = Two Note per String
3NpS = Three Note per String
4NpS = Four Note per String

Scale Grid

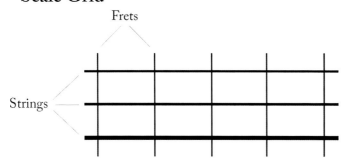

Frets

Strings

Standard Tuning Bass Tab

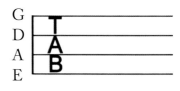

Preface

"Imagine your eyes like dancing on the notes that you want to play, and then forget about whether your hands can do it or not. Just try it!"
(Allan Holdsworth, 1992)

Like many of us, most of the legendary musicians who made the history of modern music started as self taught musicians, learning their craft by ear, practicing with passion, dedication – sometimes obsession – and trial and error.

Starting off as self taught, the only method I figured out to learn the bass guitar was trial and error whilst playing along with a music cassette – in a galaxy far, far away before internet was available to me.

The first big obstacle I encountered when I first approached the instrument was 1) finding the notes on the fretboard, and 2) moving my fingers accordingly in order to play the music I love and make it sound good.

I could see similarities between the songs and lines I was learning but, without a clear structure and a correlation between all of the elements, I had to remember a lot of notes, hand shifts and digit combinations. All the notes were like a bunch of dots scattered on the fretboard, and there were a few 'twilight zone' areas on the neck yet to be explored.

That's where Scales come in. Organising notes by interval hierarchy, scales are the basic structure of music from which all melodies, chords and harmony notes derive.

By cataloging the notes through scales, I started to connect the dots all over the fretboard, gaining more confidence and freedom by unlocking my playing, and enjoying more and more the process of learning music on my instrument.

This first volume focusses exclusively on Scales presented through the **Scale Colour System**. I developed this method over ten years of teaching, researching and experimenting with students a system that merges music theory with the mechanics of the instrument to help internalise, rather than memorise, the displacement of the note patterns over the entire fretboard.

I recommend that you follow this book with your instrument so that in any moment you can put into practice all the elements illustrated. All you need beside this book is your passion for music, determination to learn and your instrument in tune.

SCALE COLOUR SYSTEM
VISUALISE THE FRETBOARD &
UNLOCK YOUR PLAYING

Designed for guitar and bass, the **Scale Colour System** is a unique easy-to-use method to bridge the gap between the music **Theory** and the instrument **Practice**.

The original graphics and illustrations are intuitive tools to visualise and internalise the symmetry of the fretboard – a crucial aspect to mastering the instrument – and to learn music concepts through practical application.

Harmony & Theory analyses the notes and all their combinations through scales, chords and arpeggios. The note interval displacement on the fretboard will determine the most efficient *Fretting Hand* fingering to improve dexterity and develop total control of your playing.

Each concept is ordered progressively by its core principals and is presented with simple and logical step by step indications. You can start from any point in the book and easily explore all the information you need moving in any direction and build your own learning path. The versatile structure fits any level and learning preferences.

The **Scale Charts** at the end of each paragraph, and the **Glossary** at the end of this volume will serve as a summary and quick reference to address all the elements.

Levels: Beginner to Advanced.

This system aims to build a strong understanding of music theory and its application on the instrument, to fill some of the gaps that may have occurred during previous studies, and to provide another point of view to look at music.

Music concepts have no limitations, and they can be taken to any level of proficiency. All music elements are simple. Complex concepts are made out of simple elements.

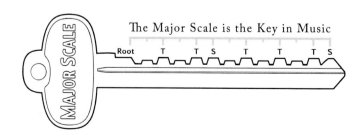

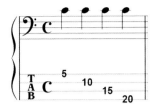

Due to the symmetrical quality of string instruments, some notes can be found in more than one area of the neck, on more than one string. As a result, remembering all the positions and shapes to combine all notes on the fretboard may be a hard task.

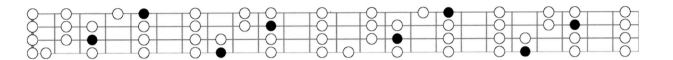

To easily visualise and learn the notes and their patterns on the instrument, the *Scale Colour System* organises the interval combinations by colour code to build and play all scales.

Tone (Red)

Semitone + Tone (Blue)

Tone + Semitone (Yellow)

Tone + Tone (Green)

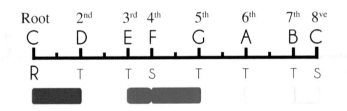

Each colour code is the construction block to build any scale on your instrument. Map and learn all notes on the fretboard by moving blocks in a *Tetris* fashion.

The colour blocks determine note alignment and the relevant digit to access all interval combinations for each scale, improving the *Fretting Hand* technique and accuracy.

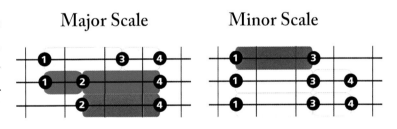

E.g. C Major Scale over the entire fretboard – includes open strings E, A, D, G.

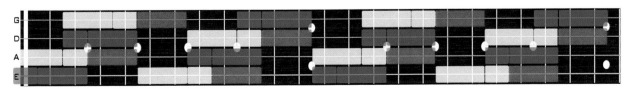

All the notes you need are already under your fingers. Use them responsibly.

1. Music Scales

"The practice of scales enables one to solve a greater number of technical problems in a shorter time than the study of any other exercise."

(Andres Segovia, 1953, p.1)

Musical scales are organised sequences of notes, ordered by pitch, and positioned at specific distances – called intervals – in relation to the starting note, the Root.

The sound and the name of scales are determined by the notes they comprise and, although they may differ in the number of notes, ranging from 5 to 12, each scale structure is repeated identically at any octave.

Scales also include the note combinations to build the harmony. The *Chord Tones* to form any *Chord* or *Arpeggio* are a selection of specific scale notes.

○━┳ The Mechanism of Notes

The symmetrical tuning system adopted in Western music uses twelve notes and is called **Equal Temperament**.

Equal Temperament finds the twelve notes we use at the intervals of twelve consecutive *fifths*. The **Circle of Fifths** represents the order in which twelve fifths come back to the starting note. The *Circle of Fifths* will be also used as a graphic reference to represent the notes featured in each scale.

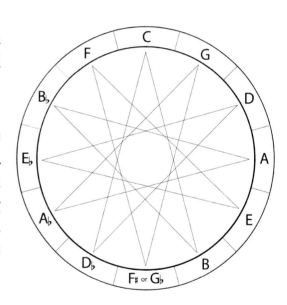

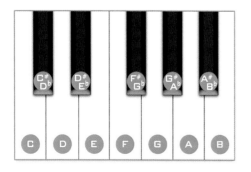

Consequently the interval of one Octave is divided into twelve equidistant notes.

Scale Forms

As Western music features only twelve notes, they can be combined together to create hundreds of scales – including all keys, modes, interval combinations and variations – however all scales can be assimilated into only **five core scale forms**.

Presenting a different number of notes per octave, scales are divided in three groups:

Heptatonic Scales (7 notes)

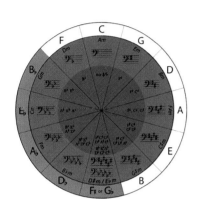

Major and Minor Scales

The Natural Minor scale is a permutation of the Major Scale. The Melodic Minor and Harmonic Minor Scales are two variations of the Major Scale.

Pentatonic Scales (5 notes)

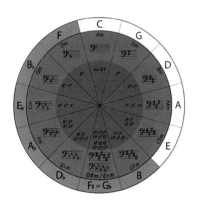

Symmetrical Scales

(6 notes)	(8 notes)	(12 notes)
Whole Tone Scale	Diminished Scales	Chromatic Scale
	Semitone-Tone/Tone-Semitone	

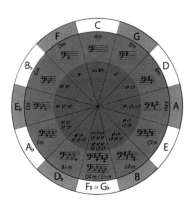 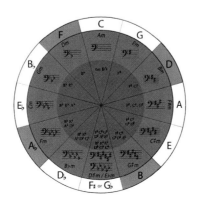 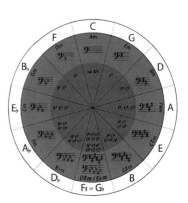

Notes, Intervals and Scales

The smallest interval distance between two notes is called a **Semitone** (S), or *Half Step*, and it corresponds to the distance of one piano key, or one fret space.

The interval of two Semitones distance is called a **Tone** (T), or *Whole Step*, corresponding to the distance of two piano keys, or two fret space.

The twelve notes we use in Western music are divided into:

seven *natural* notes: C D E F G A B

five *enharmonic* notes*: C♯/D♭ D♯/E♭ F♯/G♭ G♯/A♭ A♯/B♭

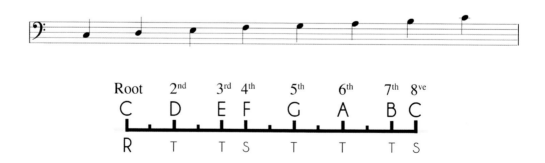

i The sequence of the seven *natural* notes starting from the note C is called **C Major Scale**. The nomenclature and interval relationship between the notes in Western music is based around this major scale and it serves as the model scale. It is a convention.

Root	2nd	3rd	4th	5th	6th	7th	8ve
C	D	E	F	G	A	B	C
R	T	T	S	T	T	T	S

* The black keys of the piano have a double name so that all *natural* notes can be raised/lowered by a Semitone – *sharp* (♯) or *flat* (♭) – to keep any scale pattern starting from any note consistent. The *enharmonic* notes are those notes that correspond to the same sound but are named in more than one way.

Intervals & Symmetry

Eight are the intervals in music, including the Root and the Octave. Organised as a mirror image, three are above the Root (*super*), and three are below the Root (*sub*).

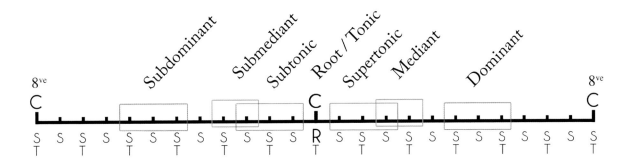

Intervals above the Root

The **2**nd note above (*super*) the Root (Tonic) is called the **Supertonic**.
The **3**rd note above the Root is called the **Mediant**.
The **5**th note above the Root is called the **Dominant**.

The **Mediant** (3rd) and the **Dominant** (5th), together with the **Root**, form the harmonic unit called *Triad*. As discussed in the **Chord & Arpeggios** volume, the Triad is the first element of Harmony creating the basic form of a chord.

Intervals below the Root

The same set of intervals above the Root are mirrored below the Root (*sub*):

the **2**nd note below the Root is called the **Subtonic** = **7**th note above the Root;
the **3**rd note below the Root is called the **Submediant** = **6**th note above the Root;
the **5**th note below the Root is called the **Subdominant** = **4**th note above the Root.

Intervals above the Octave are numbered: **9**th (2nd above the Octave), **10**th (3rd), **11**th (4th), **5**th, **13**th (6th), **7**th – they are often used to extend *Chord* and *Arpeggio Voicings*.

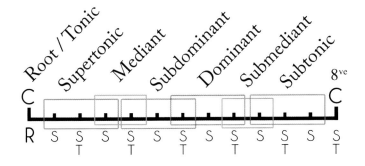

Within one octave each interval sector overlaps the previous/next by one Semitone.

Except for the Root and the Octave, the quality each interval depends on its distance from the Root. Measured in Tones and Semitones, the interval qualities determine the nature and the name of the Scale, Chord or Arpeggio they constitute.

The **Root** is the *first* interval. It is called the **Unison,** and its distance is 0 Semitones.

The 2ⁿᵈ (Supertonic) can be *Minor* (♭) / *Major* / *Augmented* (♯)

Root ♭2ⁿᵈ 2ⁿᵈ ♯2ⁿᵈ   8ᵛᵉ

R S S S S S S S S S S S

The 3ʳᵈ (Mediant) and the 6ᵗʰ (Submediant) can either be *Minor* (♭) or *Major*

Root   ♭3ʳᵈ 3ʳᵈ   ♭6ᵗʰ 6ᵗʰ   8ᵛᵉ

R S S S S S S S S S S S

The 4ᵗʰ (Subdominant) can be *Diminished* (♭) / *Perfect* / *Augmented* (♯)

Root   ♭4ᵗʰ 4ᵗʰ ♯4ᵗʰ   8ᵛᵉ

R S S S S S S S S S S S

The 5ᵗʰ (Dominant) can be *Diminished* (♭) / *Perfect* / *Augmented* (♯)

Root   ♭5ᵗʰ 5ᵗʰ ♯5ᵗʰ   8ᵛᵉ

R S S S S S S S S S S S

The 7ᵗʰ (Subtonic) can be *Minor* (♭) / *Major* or *Diminished* (♭♭)

Root   ♭♭7ᵗʰ ♭7ᵗʰ 7ᵗʰ 8ᵛᵉ

R S S S S S S S S S S S

The 8ᵛᵉ (Octave) is 12 Semitones – or 6 Tones – away from the Root.

Root   8ᵛᵉ

R S S S S S S S S S S S

Scales

The series of *natural* notes (C, D, E, F, G, A, B) starting from C is called the **C Major Scale**.

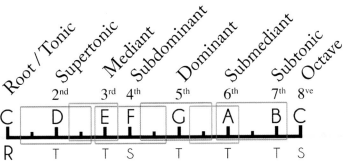

Major Scale Interval Quality

Root (Tonic) = 0 Tone (Unison)

Major 2nd = 1 Tone (Supertonic)

Major 3rd = 2 Tones (Mediant)

Perfect 4th = 2.5 Tones (Subdominant)

Perfect 5th = 3.5 Tones (Dominant)

Major 6th = 4.5 Tones (Submediant)

Major 7th = 5.5 Tones (Subtonic or *Leading Tone**)

Octave 8ve (Tonic) = 6 Tones (Unison)

* The *Major* 7th (Subtonic) is called the *Leading Tone*. Being one Semitone away form the Root or the Octave, it is the note that *leads* to the resolution – i.e. resolving to the Root.

> *i* The *major* or *minor* nature of Scales, Chords or Arpeggios, refers to and indicates only the quality of the **third** note (3rd) of the scale/chord.

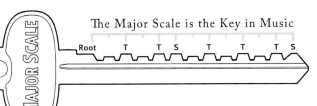

One common way to categorise and study scales is by analysing their interval sequence.

This sequence, described in Tones and Semitones, functions as a scale *blueprint* to organise and learn scale core forms, and to reproduce and transpose them in all keys using the convenient fingerings on the instrument.

Note: The interval quality identifies the order and relative distance from the Root. Intervals such as ♯/♭2nd, ♭3rd, ♯/♭4th, ♯/♭5th, ♭6th or ♭/♭♭7th do not indicate whether the specific note name is ♯ or ♭.

E.g. A Natural Minor scale features ♭3th, ♭6th and ♭7th intervals in its sequence. However it shares the very same *natural* notes of C Major Scale (A, B, C, D, E, F, G).

Root	2nd	♭3rd	4th	5th	♭6th	♭7th	8ve
A	B	C	D	E	F	G	A
R	T	S	T	T	S	T	T

The third note C is at 1.5 Tone away from the Root = *minor* 3rd (♭3rd);

The sixth note F is 4 Tones away = *minor* 6th (♭6th);

The seventh note G is 5 Tones away = *minor* 7th (♭7th).

In other words, although C is the ♭3rd of A it does not become C♭.

Similarly the fourth note of F is B = ♯4th – as it is 3 Tones away from the Root. F's *Perfect* 4th would be B♭.

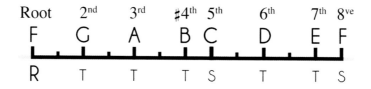

Root	2nd	3rd	♯4th	5th	6th	7th	8ve
F	G	A	B	C	D	E	F
R	T	T	T	S	T	T	S

Starting a scale sequence from a different Root will modify the order of the notes and relative interval sequence – as discussed in **The Modes of the Major Scale**.

Keys and transposition, Tonality and the use of the *enharmonic* notes (♯/♭) are discussed in **The Circle of Fifths**.

2. The Major Scale

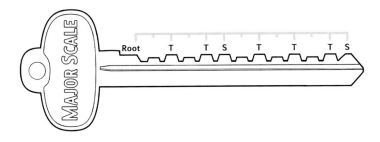

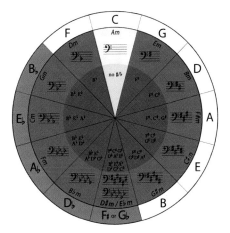

The Major Scale is a Heptatonic scale organised in a specific interval series (Diatonic). The name *Heptatonic* comes from the Greek word *Eptá* (επτά) meaning seven. *Diatonic* indicates that the scale presents two *Semitone* intervals separated by either two or three consecutive *whole Tone* intervals.

The C Major scale offers the best example to start learning notes and scales as their organisation and nomenclature revolves around this scale.

The notes of the C Major scale are called *natural* and correspond to the white keys of the piano keyboard: **C D E F G A B** and **C** (to complete one octave).

The *enharmonic* notes on the black keys (♯ or ♭) make a semitone gap between some of the *natural* notes, creating the specific interval series of the Major Scale:

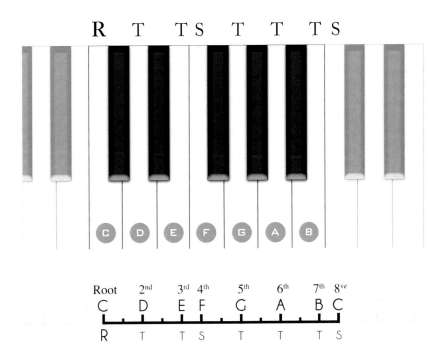

C Major scale notated in bass clef:

One Finger per fret Position (1Fpf) – Red, Blue, Yellow

You might be familiar with this shape representing one common major scale position. The numbered dots indicate the suggested F.H. digit for each block.

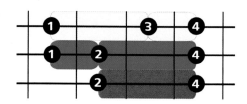

As each colour block corresponds to one portion of the Major Scale sequence, like building blocks they can be stacked vertically or aligned horizontally to move the notes across the fretboard.

Example 1: One octave C Major scale in one position across three strings.

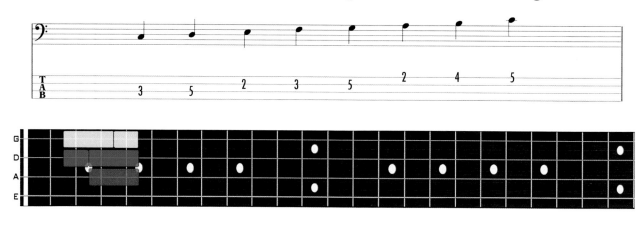

In terms of intervals, it is important to notice that all **Red**, **Blue** and **Yellow** blocks are one Tone away from each other.

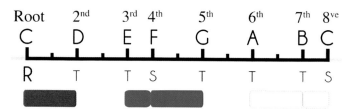

Two notes one Tone apart can either be two frets away on the same string (C-D); or three frets away on the adjacent string – covering a space of four frets **1Fpf** (D-E).

This means that each block can be shifted over the fretboard, to extend and displace the notes of the scale on any string and in any direction.

The symmetry of the fretboard allows you to find the same notes by shifting blocks horizontally.

Example 2: One octave C Major scale in two positions across two strings.

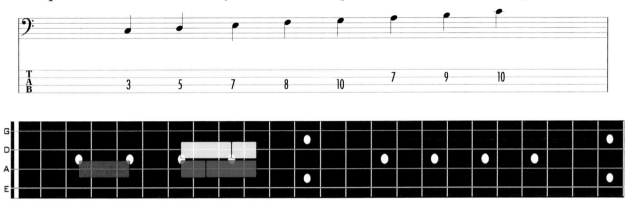

Displacing the notes on one string is a good way to learn the fretboard and familiarise oneself with all areas of the neck.

Example 3: One octave C Major scale in three positions over one string.

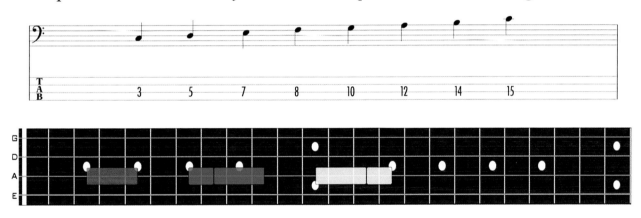

The displacement of all scale notes on the instrument will look clearer once all block structures are moved over the entire fretboard.

Example 4: C Major Scale on the entire fretboard – include open strings E, A, D, G.

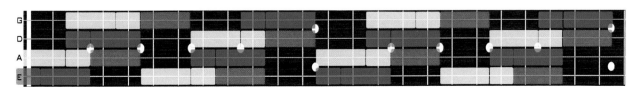

Stretched Position, Five frets per String – Green, Green, Blue

The Major Scale intervals can also be arranged by two Tones (**Green block**) – stretching one F.H. finger to cover a space of five fret on one string (**5fpS**). A common position for guitarists, this may be more demanding on the bass – use with caution.

By covering a bigger interval, this position is particularly convenient to quickly move to the upper register of the fretboard.

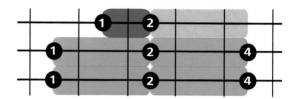

The distance between the **Green** blocks is now of one Semitone, as the stretched position covers one extra fret space – i.e. one extra Tone every two blocks.

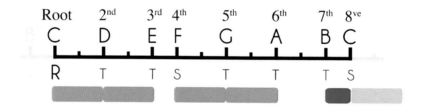

Note: The digit for the last two notes (B and C) is presented as a partial **Blue** block. To optimise the use of the F.H., the interval of one Semitone is always associated with the previous/following Tone block.

Example 5: One octave C Major scale in one position across three strings (**5fpS**).

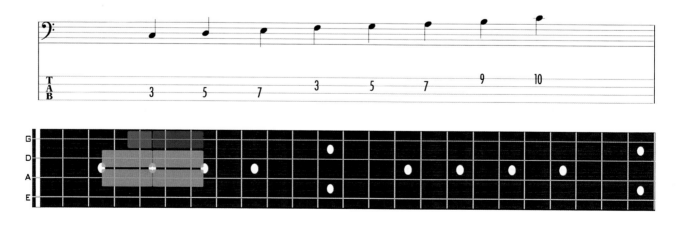

Example 6: One octave C Major scale in two positions across two strings (**5fpS**).

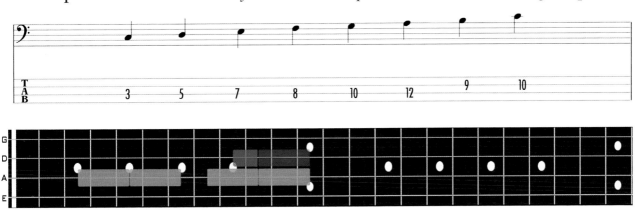

Note: While **Red**, **Blue** and **Yellow** blocks are always <u>one Tone away from any block</u>, the **Green** blocks are displaced at the distance of just one Semitone.

Example 7: One octave C Major scale in three positions over one strings (**5fpS**).

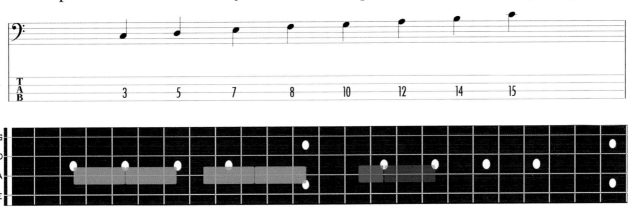

Note: The **Blue** block in *Examples 5, 6* and *7*, incorporates the **Red** block of *Examples 1, 2, 3* and *4*.

Corresponding to one Tone interval, **Red blocks can turn into any other colour** depending on the notes they are next to, and your digit choice.

i.e. **Green** is two consecutive **Reds**; **Blue** and **Yellow** are one **Red** plus a Semitone.

A deeper analysis of the Major Scale is discussed in **The Modes of the Major Scale**.

<u>Learn all the notes on the fretboard</u>
to play with awareness and to
improve your technique.

3. The Modes of the Major Scale

The Modes of the Major Scale are the seven interval permutations starting from each scale degree.

From each of the seven notes of the Major Scale – any major scale – we can build seven scales with different qualities and characteristics. These scales are called **Modes** and Mode I is the Major Scale. Because the note displacement changes depending on the note we start the scale from, each mode has a unique colour and interval structure.

As the Major Scale note sequence **R T T S T T T S** repeats itself in each octave, we can identify seven permutations of this sequence starting from each degree of the scale.

I) Ionian (Major Scale)

```
    C   D   E F   G   A   B C
    R   T   T S   T   T   T S
```

II) Dorian

```
    D   E F   G   A   B C   D
    R   T S   T   T   T S   T
```

III) Phrygian

```
    E F   G   A   B C   D   E
    R S   T   T   T S   T   T
```

IV) Lydian

```
    F   G   A   B C   D   E F
    R   T   T   T S   T   T S
```

V) Mixolydian

```
    G   A   B C   D   E F   G
    R   T   T S   T   T S   T
```

VI) Aeolian (Natural Minor Scale)

```
    A   B C   D   E F   G   A
    R   T S   T   T S   T   T
```

VII) Locrian

```
    B C   D   E F   G   A   B
    R S   T   T S   T   T   T
```

The degrees represent and identify the notes and their position inside the scale. Ordered in Roman numerals, the degrees of the Major Scale are seven, starting from the first note (Root).

Referencing the C Major scale we find:

C = Root – I degree
D = 2nd – II degree
E = 3rd – III degree
F = 4th – IV degree
G = 5th – V degree
A = 6th – VI degree
B = 7th – VII degree
C = 8ve – I degree

Each mode is associated with a grade of the Major Scale and each one of them generates a type of chord or arpeggio related to its intervals (**Chord Tones**).
Chords and arpeggios are discussed in **Volume 2 – Arpeggios & Chords**.

Because each mode is basically a portion of the Major Scale, they are seven combinations of the same *Scale Colour System* blocks applied to **The Major Scale** – as seen in the previous pages.

The seven modes combined together provide all position combinations to play all the notes available in a specific key – e.g. C Major, G Major, B♭ Major etc.

All of the following examples will be in the key of C Major – as it does not include any *sharps* (♯) or *flats* (♭). Once the Major Scale and its Modes are learnt in one key, it will be easier to transpose them in all keys because of the transposing nature of the instrument. Keys and transposition are discussed in **The Circle of Fifths** section.

What follows is the list of the seven Major Scale Modes with names, intervals and relative *Scale Colour System* code, followed by the Modes Chart diagrams – for both one finger per fret (**1Fpf**) and five frets per string stretched positions (**5fpS**).

I) **IONIAN** – Red, Blue, Yellow
   (Major Scale)

The Ionian is the first of the Major Scale Modes. It features seven notes displaced at the specific distance **R T T S T T T S** and its intervals are:

Root

2nd = Major

3rd = Major

4th = Perfect

5th = Perfect

6th = Major

7th = Major

8^{ve}

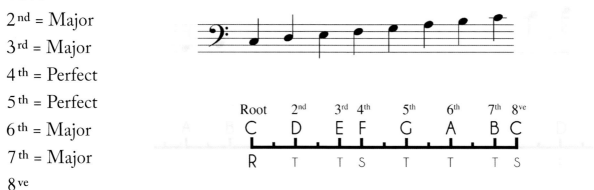

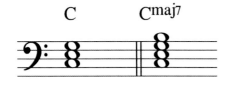

The **Root**, 3rd, 5th of the Ionian mode form a **Major Triad** chord or arpeggio (C, E, G). Adding the 7th creates a **Major7** chord or arpeggio (C, E, G, B).

Colour code for **1Fpf** and **5fpS*** positions. The dots represent the scale intervals.

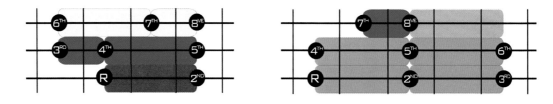

C Ionian, **1Fpf** position, one octave – starting on C at fret *III* of the A string.

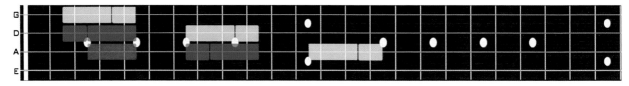

C Ionian, **1Fpf** position over the entire fretboard – includes open strings E, A, D, G.

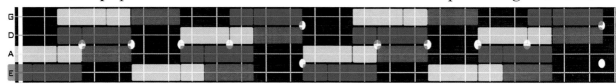

*5fpS positions are discussed in the **Colour Block Formula** at the end of this section.

II) **DORIAN** – Yellow, Red, Blue

The Dorian is the second of the Major Scale Modes. It features seven notes displaced at the specific distance **R T S T T T S T** and its intervals are:

Root

2ⁿᵈ = Major

♭3ʳᵈ = Minor

4ᵗʰ = Perfect

5ᵗʰ = Perfect

6ᵗʰ = Major

♭7ᵗʰ = Minor

8ᵛᵉ

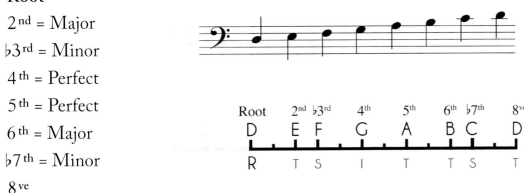

The **Root**, ♭3ʳᵈ, 5ᵗʰ of the Dorian mode form a **Minor Triad** chord or arpeggio (D, F, A). Adding the ♭7ᵗʰ creates a **Minor 7** chord or arpeggio (D, F, A, C).

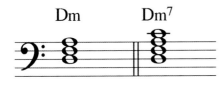

Colour code for **1Fpf** and **5fpS*** positions. The dots represent the scale intervals.

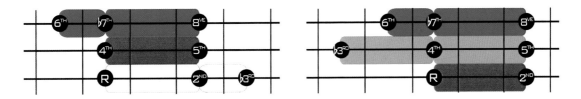

D Dorian, **1Fpf** position, one octave – starting on D at fret *V* of the A string.

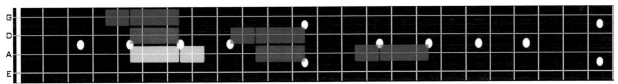

D Dorian, **1Fpf** position over the entire fretboard – includes open strings E, A, D, G.

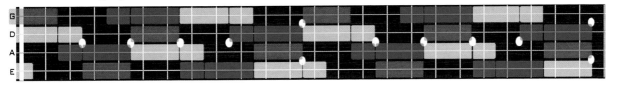

***5fpS** positions are discussed in the **Colour Block Formula** at the end of this section.

III) **PHRYGIAN** – Blue, Yellow, Red

The Phrygian is the third of the Major Scale Modes. It features seven notes displaced at the specific distance **R S T T T S T T** and its intervals are:

Root

♭2nd = Minor

♭3rd = Minor

4th = Perfect

5th = Perfect

♭6th = Minor

♭7th = Minor

8^{ve}

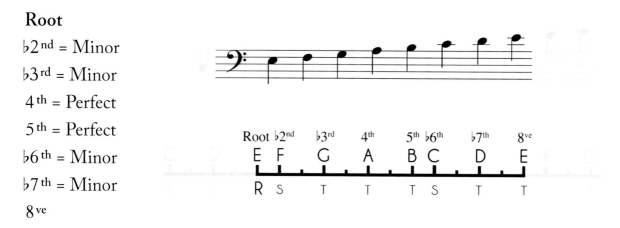

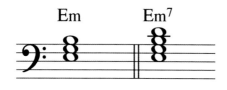

The **Root**, ♭3rd, 5th of the Phrygian mode form a **Minor Triad** chord or arpeggio (E, G, B). Adding the ♭7th creates a **Minor 7** chord or arpeggio (E, G, B, D).

Colour code for **1Fpf** and **5fpS*** positions. The dots represent the scale intervals.

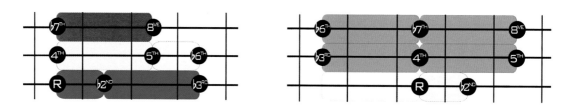

E Phrygian, **1Fpf** position, one octave – starting on E at fret *VII* of the A string.

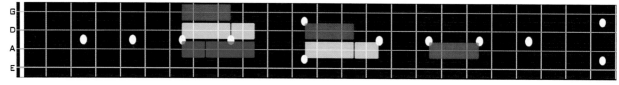

E Phrygian, **1Fpf** position on the entire fretboard – includes open strings E, A, D, G.

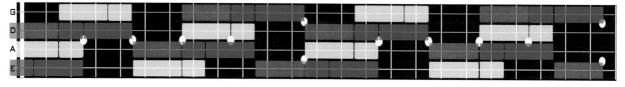

*****5fpS** positions are discussed in the **Colour Block Formula** at the end of this section.

IV) **LYDIAN** – Red, Yellow, Yellow

The Lydian is the fourth of the Major Scale Modes. It features seven notes displaced at the specific distance **R T T T S T T S** and its intervals are:

Root
2nd = Major
3rd = Major
♯4th = Augmented
5th = Perfect
6th = Major
7th = Major
8ve

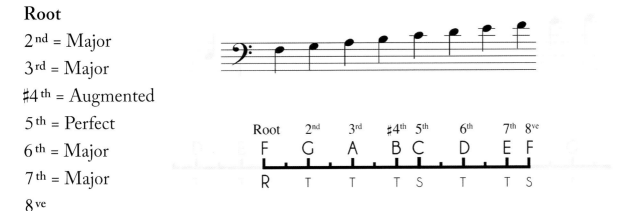

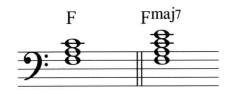

The **Root**, 3rd, 5th of the Lydian mode form a **Major Triad** chord or arpeggio (F, A, C). Adding the 7th creates a **Major7** chord or arpeggio (F, A, C, E).

Colour code for **1Fpf** and **5fpS*** positions. The dots represent the scale intervals.

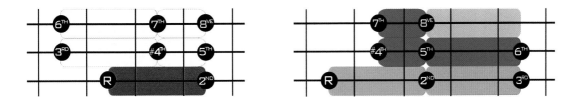

F Lydian, **1Fpf** position, one octave – starting on F at fret *VIII* of the A string.

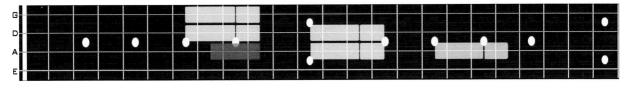

F Lydian, **1Fpf** position over the entire fretboard – includes open strings E, A, D, G.

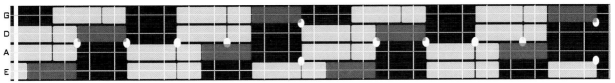

*5fpS positions are discussed in the **Colour Block Formula** at the end of this section.

V) **MIXOLYDIAN** – Red, Blue, Blue

The Mixolydian is the fifth of the Major Scale Modes. It features seven notes displaced at the specific distance **R T T S T T S T** and its intervals are:

Root

2nd = Major

3rd = Major

4th = Perfect

5th = Perfect

6th = Major

♭7th = Minor

8^{ve}

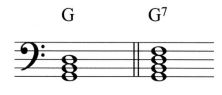

The **Root**, 3rd, 5th of the Mixolydian mode form a **Major Triad** chord or arpeggio (G, B, D). Adding the ♭7th creates a **7** chord or arpeggio (G, B, D, F).

Colour code for **1Fpf** and **5fpS*** positions. The dots represent the scale intervals.

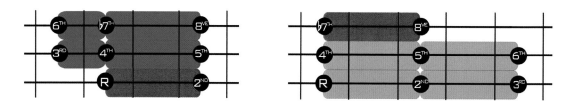

G Mixolydian, **1Fpf** position, one octave – starting on G at fret *III* of the E string.

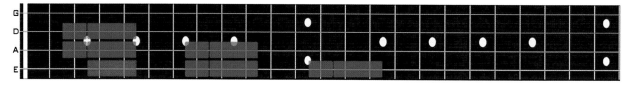

G Mixolydian, **1Fpf** over the entire fretboard – includes open strings E, A, D, G.

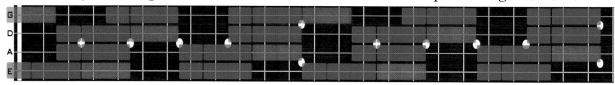

*5fpS positions are discussed in the **Colour Block Formula** at the end of this section.

VI) **AEOLIAN** – Yellow, Yellow, Red
(Natural Minor Scale)

The Aeolian is the sixth of the Major Scale Modes. It features seven notes displaced at the specific distance **R T S T T S T T** and its intervals are:

Root

2nd = Major

♭3rd = Minor

4th = Perfect

5th = Perfect

♭6th = Minor

♭7th = Minor

8^{ve}

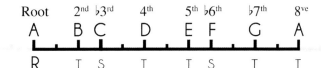

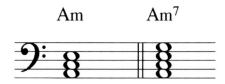

The **Root**, ♭3rd, 5th of the Aeolian mode form a **Minor Triad** chord or arpeggio (A, C, E). Adding the ♭7th creates a **Minor 7** chord or arpeggio (A, C, E, G).

Colour code for **1Fpf** and **5fpS*** positions. The dots represent the scale intervals.

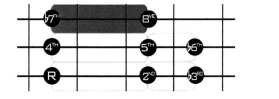
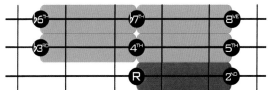

A Aeolian, **1Fpf** position, one octave – starting on A at fret *V* of the E string.

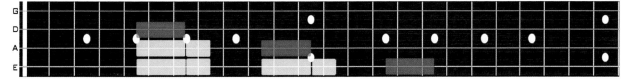

A Aeolian, **1Fpf** position on the entire fretboard – includes open strings E, A, D, G.

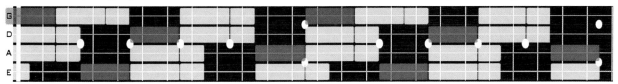

*5fpS positions are discussed in the **Colour Block Formula** at the end of this section.

VII) **LOCRIAN** – Blue, Blue, Red

The Locrian is the seventh of the Major Scale Modes. It features seven notes displaced at the specific distance **R S T T S T T T** and its intervals are:

Root

♭2ⁿᵈ = Minor

♭3ʳᵈ = Minor

4ᵗʰ = Perfect

♭5ᵗʰ = Diminished

♭6ᵗʰ = Minor

♭7ᵗʰ = Minor

8ᵛᵉ

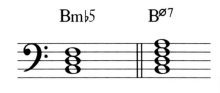

The **Root, ♭3ʳᵈ, ♭5ᵗʰ** of the Locrian mode form a **Diminished Triad** chord/arpeggio (B, D, F). Adding the ♭7ᵗʰ creates a **Minor 7♭5 (ø)** chord/arpeggio (B, D, F, A).

Colour code for **1Fpf** and **5fpS*** positions. The dots represent the scale intervals.

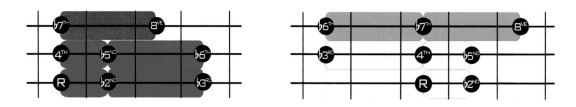

B Locrian, **1Fpf** position, one octave – starting on B at fret *II* of the A string.

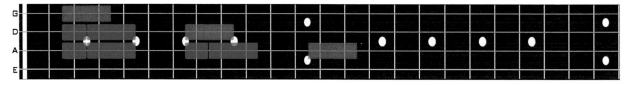

B Locrian, **1Fpf** position on the entire fretboard – includes open strings E, A, D, G.

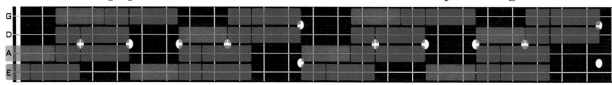

*5fpS positions are discussed in the **Colour Block Formula** at the end of this section.

Major Scale Colour Block Formula

Because the Major Scale has a fixed series of intervals, all Major Scale colour blocks combinations follow two master colour block "formulas" – <u>starting from the V degree of the Major Scale</u>. The positions of all Modes are included in:

Red, Blue, Blue, Yellow, Yellow for the 1Fpf position.

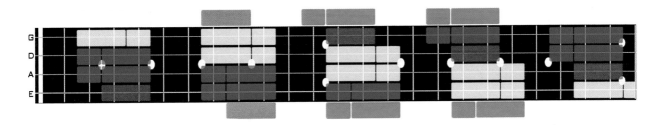

Green, Green, Green, Blue, Blue, Yellow, Yellow – 5fpS, stretched position.

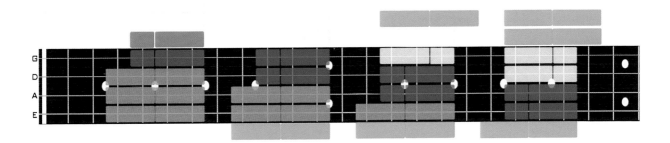

These two sequences are very useful to extend the scale of each Mode both vertically and horizontally on the neck – e.g. shifting position to play a two octave scale – and to visualise how Mode positions merge into each other's blocks.

> *i*
>
> In the Major Scale: **Red, Blue** and **Yellow** blocks are always one tone away from any block. The three **Green** blocks are displaced at one semitone distance from each other – as they start on the very next fret.

Understanding how the scale patterns develop over the entire fretboard is vital for transposing scales in all keys, as the whole interval grid moves altogether – is notched down a string when moving keys up a fifth (C to G, D, A, E etc.), and one string up when moving down a fifth (C to F, B♭, E♭ etc.) – as showed in **The Circle of Fifths**.

C Major Scale Modes

Major Scale Modes: combinations of **Red**, **Blue**, **Yellow** and **Green** blocks.

I) C Ionian (Major Scale)

II) D Dorian

III) E Phrygian

IV) F Lydian

V) G Mixolydian

VI) A Aeolian (Natural Minor)

VII) B Locrian

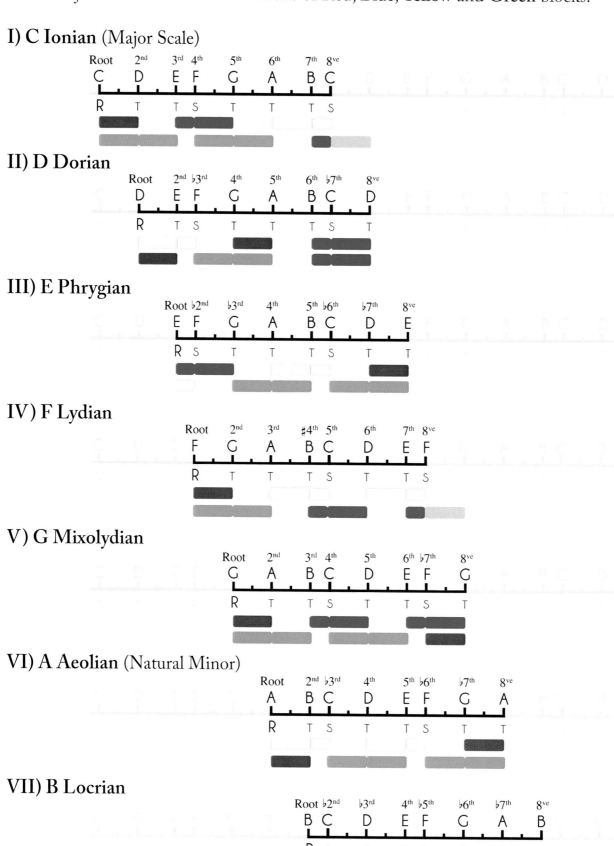

Major Scale – Modes Chart

The numbered dots represent the suggested Fretting Hand fingering.

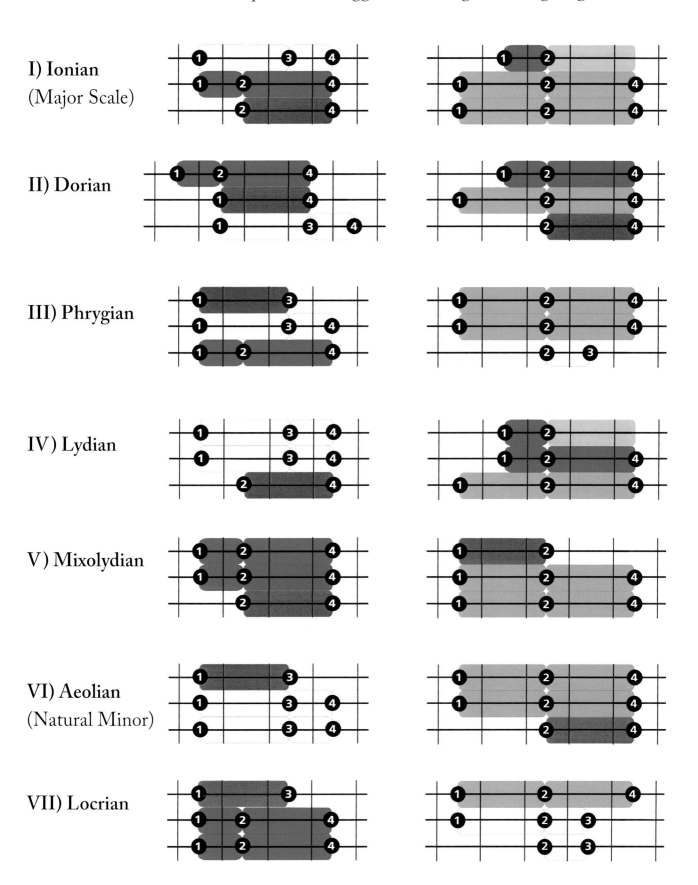

I) Ionian
(Major Scale)

II) Dorian

III) Phrygian

IV) Lydian

V) Mixolydian

VI) Aeolian
(Natural Minor)

VII) Locrian

4. The Circle of Fifths
& the Key concept of Music

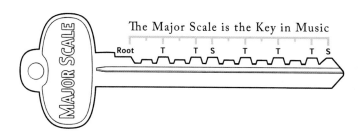

Because the symmetry of the tuning system adopted in Western music (Equal Temperament) is built around the interval of a fifth, we find that after a *cycle* of twelve consecutive *fifths* we reach the note we started from.

The notes we use in music are exactly these twelve fifths – wisely arranged into octaves.

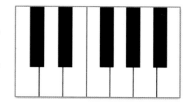

The **Circle of Fifths** simply represents the order of the twelve fifths. The Major Scale built on each one of them is called **Key**, or Tonal Centre, and it is used in music to identify a specific group of notes.

The *Circle of Fifth* is a key concept in music recurring in more than one instance.

As a consequence, each key around the circle presents an increasing number of ♯/♭. Needless to say that the Major Scale develops its own Modes in each key – as seen in **The Modes of the Major Scale.**

The concept of **Tonality*** is *relative* to two specific Modes of the Major Scale: Mode **I** and Mode **VI**.

These two relative modes represent the two *moods* of the Major Scale. Mode I being *bright* and *cheerful*, and Mode VI *darker* and more *contemplative*, one is the relative minor or major tonality of each other.

** Because **both tonalities look the same** when written in notation, it is always good to distinguish them to know around which of the two modes the music revolves around.*

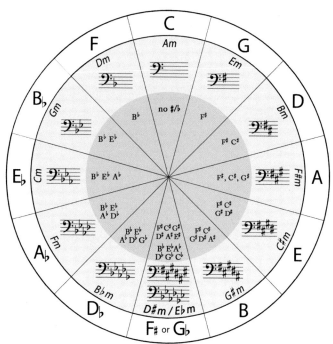

To understand the behaviour of the scales when transposing key, and the use of ♯ and ♭ notes, it is useful – once again – to focus on the Major Scale construction.

The Key transposition revolves around three degrees and relative Modes of the Major Scale: Mode **I**, Mode **IV**, and Mode **V**.

Starting the *Circle of Fifths* from the *zero point* key of **C** – as it includes only natural notes (C, D, E, F, G, A, B, C), therefore having zero ♯/♭ – keys are transposed by moving up a fifth – C to G (V degree) – or down a fifth – C to F (IV degree).

This implies that the scale built on those two degrees has to match the intervals of the Major Scale – which functions as a Major Scale model (Mode I – **Ionian**).

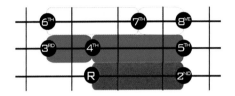

Moving Up a fifth (adding ♯)

The **G Mixolydian** scale (Mode V) matches all intervals of the Major Scale but one: the ♭7th (F). Raising this note by one semitone (F♯) will turn the *Blue* block into a *Yellow* block – hence a Major Scale and the new Key. G Major (G, A, B, C, D, E, <u>F♯</u>, G).

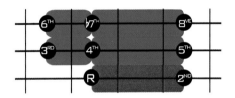

Moving Down a fifth (adding ♭)

The **F Lydian** scale (Mode IV) matches all intervals of the Ionian mode but one: the ♯4th (B). Lowering this note by one semitone (B♭) will turn the *Yellow* block into a *Blue* block – hence a Major Scale and the new Key. F Major (F, G, A, <u>B♭</u>, C, D, E, F).

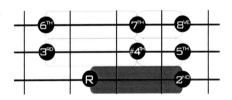

One more ♯ or ♭ will be added to the following keys when moving by one fifth – where each ♭7th will be sharpened when ascending, and each ♯4th will be flattened when descending.

Note: In notation ♯ and ♭ are notated following the specific order displayed in the Circle of Fifths – each key implies the alterations of the previous ones.

Enharmonic Notes

As introduced in the **Music Scales**, the Enharmonic Notes are all those notes that correspond to the same sound, but are named in more than one way.

The notes – and relative keys - presented in the *Circle of Fifth* are the seven *natural* notes (C, D, E, F, G, A, B) and five *flat* notes (B♭, E♭, A♭, D♭, G♭) – one of which overlaps with one *sharp* key (G♭ or F♯).

The keys of C♯, D♯, G♯, A♯ are not listed because those sounds are enharmonic to the ♭ keys in the *Circle of Fifths*.

E.g.

 While the key of **C♯** Major would have seven ♯ notes, as all C Major scale notes are raised by one semitone –

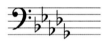 the enharmonic key of **D♭** has five ♭ (two fewer alterations than **C♯**).

The key of **G♯** will feature six ♯ and one *double sharp* (F𝄪):

A♭ major instead features only four *flats*: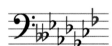

 The key of F♭, to get back to the *enharmonic relativity formula* above, would involve six ♭ and one *double flat* (♭♭).

The tendency – which has become a convention – is to include the least number of ♯ and ♭ in the key. Although they sound the same, the Enharmonic notes are used to facilitate the recognition and clarify the structure of the notes belonging to a scale.

Now I turn the question at the top to you:

Is = ?

All the notes in the scale correspond to a precise interval and have a relevance and function in the harmony. It is advisable to identify and name them properly also because ♯ and ♭ are indicative for the key and the nature of the scale itself.

When studying any scale in any key, pay attention to the note sequence and make sure they are named properly and none of them is missing from the series.

Accidentals are the temporary alterations. They happen in music when a note in a specific key needs to be *sharpened* or *flattened* momentarily. In fact the alteration lasts until the end of the bar in which it occurs – in the following bar all accidentals disappear and the note returns to its designated place.

In notation however, a friendly *natural* symbol (♮) is often used to remind that the note altered in the previous bar has returned natural.

In this example in D Major, the note G becomes *sharp* (♯) in the second half of bar 1 and returns natural in bar 2.

If a note is ♯ or ♭ for the whole piece, or a section of it, generally it is included in the relevant set key.

Getting around the fretboard

The transposing nature of stringed instruments allows you to move from one key to another more easily than on wind or keyboard instruments. This operation however, may not seem as intuitive as it looks – it requires a deep understanding of notes, intervals and positions on the fretboard.

Below are the full fretboard *Scale Colour Systems* of the Major Scale for all twelve keys to point out one simple mechanical aspect of the fretboard: **the whole interval grid shifts vertically.**

– <u>one string below</u> when moving <u>up a fifth</u> (i.e. C to G),

– <u>one string above</u> when moving <u>down a fifth</u> (i.e. C to F).

C Major

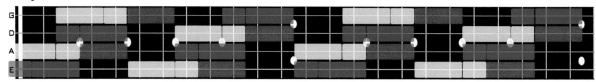

G Major

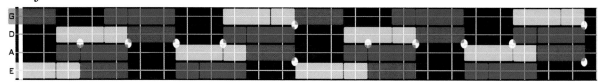

D Major

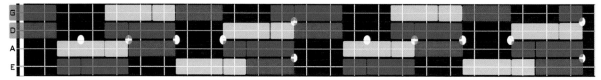

A Major

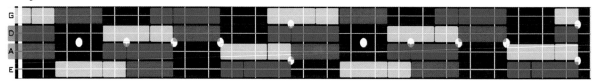

E Major

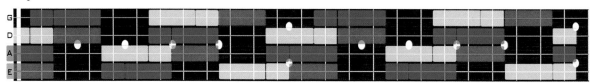

B Major

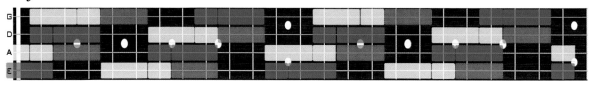

F♯ or G♭ Major

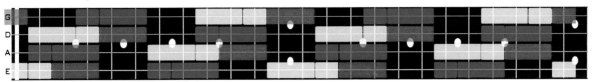

D♭ Major

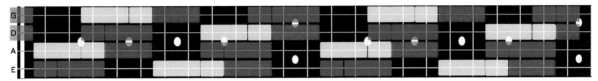

A♭ Major

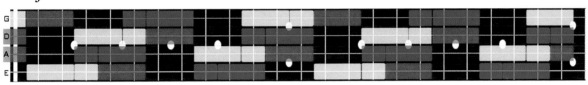

E♭ Major

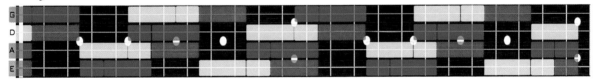

B♭ Major

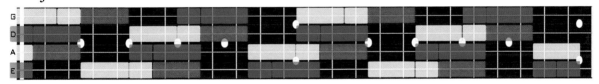

F Major

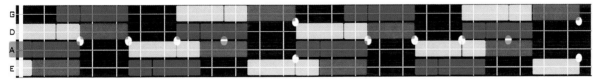

C Major

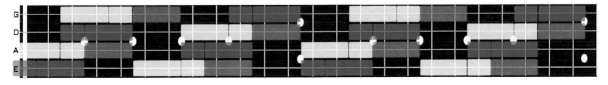

Major Scale and Relative Minor Scale

Amongst the Modes of the Major Scale there are two scales in particular which have been greatly exploited in music, the *Major Scale* (Ionian – Mode I) and the *Minor Scale* (Aeolian – Mode VI).

When a piece of music is in a *major* key it revolves around the Major Scale and tends to resolve on its tonic. Instead when the tonality is *minor*, it revolves around the Minor Scale.

These two scales are preferred to the other modes and particularly suitable for the development of motifs as they are the only two modes presenting a consistent form of major or minor triads built on their grades I, IV and V (Schenker, 1954).

	SUBDOMINANT (IV)	TONIC (I)	DOMINANT (V)
Ionian (Major Scale)	F major	C major	G major
Aeolian (Minor Scale)	Dm minor	Am minor	Em minor

As the *minor* scale (Mode VI) derives from the *major* scale (Mode I), one is relative to the other and they share the same number of alterations (♯, ♭) – see **The Circle of Fifths**.

Major Scale (C)   Minor Scale (Am)

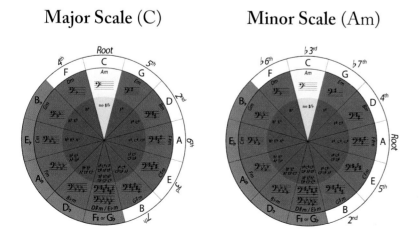

Every Major Scale has a *relative* Minor Scale built on its sixth degree. Every Minor Scale has a *relative* Major Scale built on its third degree.

5. Minor Scales

In contrast to the Major Scale, which only appears in one form, there are three types of minor scales: the **Natural Minor**, the **Melodic Minor** and the **Harmonic Minor**.

These three minor scales belong to the *Heptatonic* scale group (each presenting 7 notes), and are permutations (Natural Minor) or variations of the Major Scale interval series (Melodic Minor and Harmonic Minor).

While the **Natural Minor Scale** is a permutation of the Major Scale – as it derives from the Major Scale interval series R T T S T T T S (*Diatonic*) – the **Melodic Minor Scale** and the **Harmonic Minor Scale** intervals differ from the *Diatonic* series by one semitone, generating their own modes and relevant harmony.

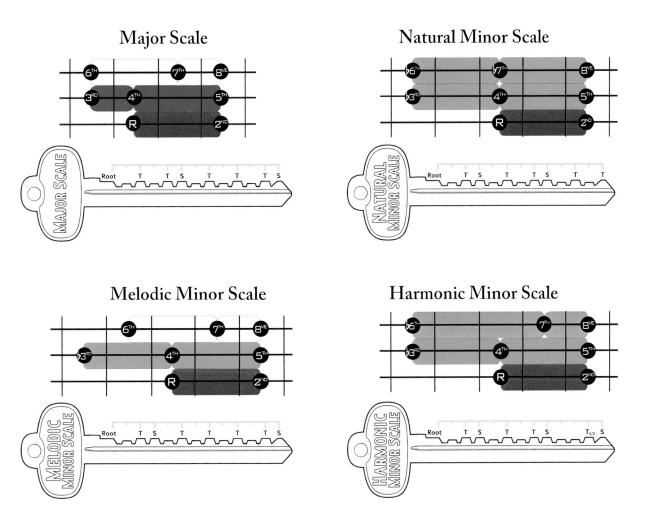

The **Melodic Minor Scale** can be seen as a Major Scale with a Minor 3rd ($\flat$3rd), the **Harmonic Minor Scale** is a Natural Minor Scale with the major 7th (leading tone).

6. The Melodic Minor Scale

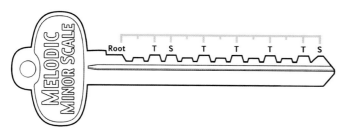

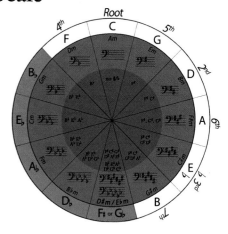

Resembling the Major Scale core form, the Melodic Minor Scale has its third degree lowered by a Semitone – resulting in a Minor 3rd (♭3rd).

The C Melodic Minor scale offers the best example to start learning this scale as it features only one *flat* note (♭): **C D E♭ F G A B** and **C** (to complete one octave).

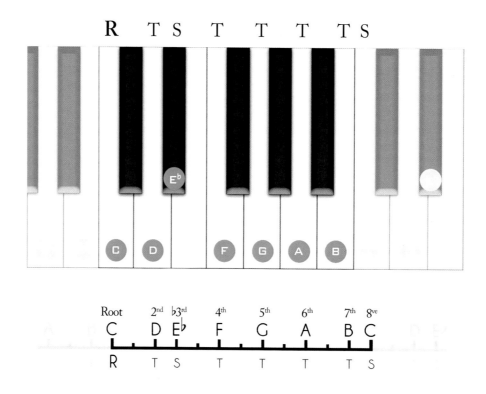

C Melodic Minor scale notated in bass clef *:

* In classical music theory the Melodic Minor Scale presents two forms: ascending as a Melodic Minor, and descending as a Natural Minor. In the following chapters it will be presented with a consistent ascending/descending structure – as it is used to be called *Jazz Melodic Minor Scale*, or *Jazz Minor Scale*.

One Finger per fret Position (1Fpf) – Yellow, Red, Yellow

The numbered dots indicate the suggested F.H. digit for each block.

As each colour block corresponds to one portion of the Melodic Minor Scale sequence, like building blocks they can be both stacked vertically or aligned horizontally to move the notes across the fretboard.

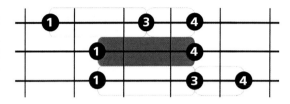

C Melodic Minor scale in three positions, starting on C at fret *III* of the A string.

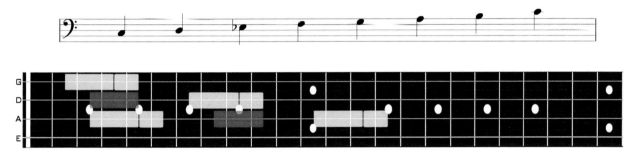

In terms of intervals, it is important to notice the **Yellow** and **Red** blocks are <u>one Tone away from each other</u>.

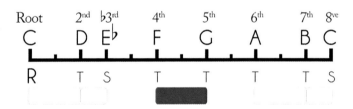

Two notes one Tone apart can either be two frets away on the same string (C-D); or three frets away on the adjacent string – covering a space of four frets **1Fpf** (E♭-F).

The symmetry of the fretboard allows you to find the same notes by shifting blocks horizontally. This means that each block can be shifted over the fretboard, to extend and displace the notes of the scale on any string and in any direction.

Stretched Position, Five frets per String – Red, Green, Yellow

The Melodic Minor Scale intervals can also be arranged with a two whole Tones block (**Green**) – stretching one F.H. finger to cover a space of five fret on one string (**5fpS**). A common position for guitarists, it can be more demanding on the bass – use with caution.

This stretched position is particularly convenient as it allows you to play the scale without moving the hand.

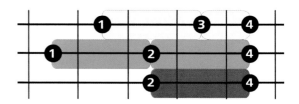

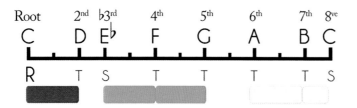

The distance between the **Red** and **Green** blocks is one Semitone, as the stretched position covers one extra fret space.

C Melodic Minor scale in three positions, starting on C at fret *III* of the A string.

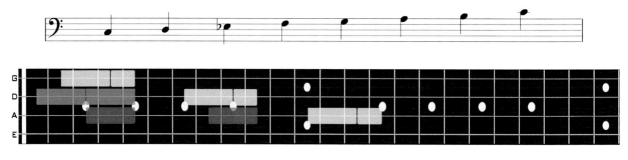

C Melodic Minor scale on the entire fretboard – include open strings A, D, G.

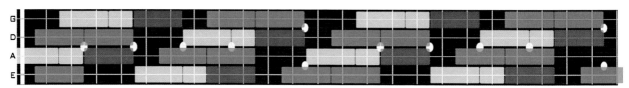

Note: The **Green** blocks are one Semitone away form the **Red** block, and one Tone from the **Yellow** blocks. The end of the **Yellow** blocks corresponds to the beginning of the **Red**.

A deeper analysis of the Melodic Minor Scale is discussed in **The Modes of the Melodic Minor Scale.**

7. The Harmonic Minor Scale

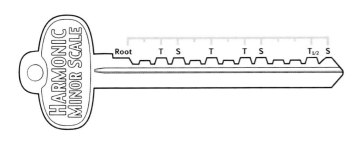

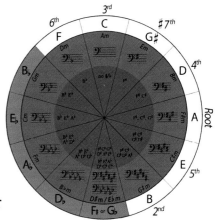

The Harmonic Minor, resembling the Natural Minor Scale core form, has its seventh degree raised up by a Semitone – resulting in a Major 7th (leading tone).

A Harmonic Minor scale offers the best example to start learning this scale as it features only one *sharp* note (♯): **A B C D E F G♯** and **A** (to complete one octave).

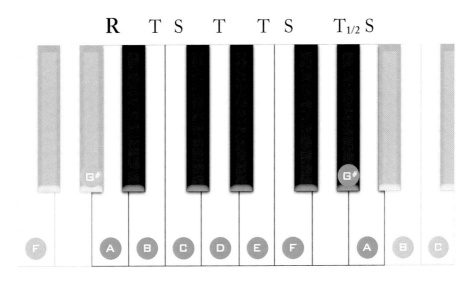

A Harmonic Minor scale notated in bass clef:

One Finger per fret Position (1Fpf) – Yellow, Yellow, Blue

The numbered dots indicate the suggested F.H. digit for each block.

As each colour block corresponds to one portion of the Harmonic Minor Scale, like building blocks they can be both stacked vertically or aligned horizontally to move the notes across the fretboard.

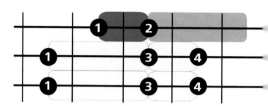

A Harmonic Minor scale in three positions, starting on A at fret *V* of the E string.

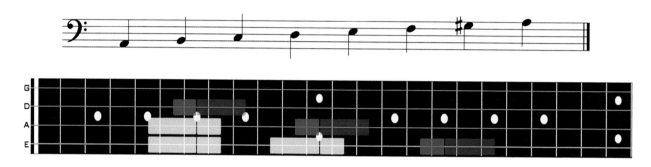

In terms of intervals, it is important to notice the **Yellow** blocks are <u>one Tone away from each other</u>. The **Blue** block is <u>one Tone and a half</u> away ($T_{1/2}$).

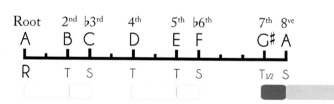

Two notes one $T_{1/2}$ apart can either be three frets away on the same string, or two frets away on the adjacent string (F-G$\sharp$).

The symmetry of the fretboard allows you to find the same notes by shifting blocks horizontally. This means that each block can be shifted over the fretboard, to extend and displace the notes of the scale on any string and in any direction.

Stretched Position, Five frets per String – Red, Green, Orange

The Harmonic Minor Scale intervals can also be arranged involving a stretched position: two whole Tones (**Green** block) and one $T_{1/2}$ + **Semitone** (**Orange** block) – covering a space of five fret on one string (**5fpS**). A common position for guitarists, it can be more demanding on the bass – use with caution.

This stretched position allows to play the scale without moving the hand. The numbered dots represent the suggested F.H. fingering.

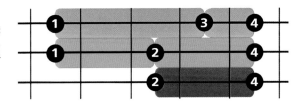

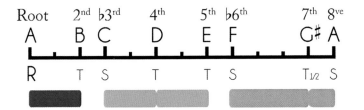

The distance between the **Red, Green** and the **Orange** is one Semitone.

A Harmonic Minor scale in three positions, starting on A at fret *V* of the E string.

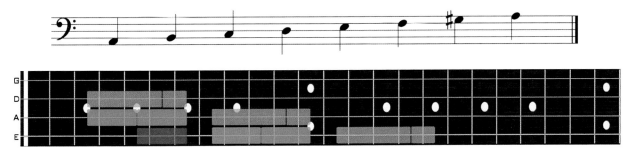

A Harmonic Minor scale on the entire fretboard – include open strings E, A and D.

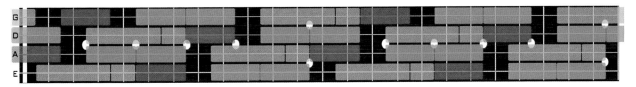

Note: All blocks, **Green**, **Red** and **Orange**, are one Semitone away from each other. The end of the **Orange** blocks corresponds to the beginning of the **Red**.

A deeper analysis of the Harmonic Minor Scale is discussed in **The Modes of the Harmonic Minor Scale.**

8. The Modes of the Melodic Minor Scale

The Modes of the Melodic Minor Scale are the seven interval permutations starting from each scale degree.

From each of the seven notes of the Melodic Scale we can build seven scales with different qualities and characteristics. These scales are called **Modes** and Mode I is the Melodic Minor Scale. Because the note displacement changes depending on the note we start the scale from, each mode has a unique colour and interval structure.

As the Minor Melodic Scale note sequence **R T S T T T T S** repeats itself in each octave, we can identify seven permutations of this sequence starting from each degree of the scale.

I) Melodic Minor

```
C   D Eb  F   G   A   B C
R   T  S  T   T   T   T S
```

II) Dorian ♭2

```
D Eb  F   G   A   B C   D
R  S  T   T   T   T S   T
```

III) Lydian Augmented

```
Eb  F   G   A   B C   D Eb
R   T   T   T   T S   T  S
```

IV) Lydian Dominant

```
F   G   A   B C   D Eb  F
R   T   T   T S   T  S  T
```

V) Mixolydian ♭6

```
G   A   B C   D Eb  F   G
R   T   T S   T  S  T   T
```

VI) Locrian ♯2

```
A   B C   D Eb  F   G   A
R   T S   T  S  T   T   T
```

VII) Altered Scale

```
B C   D Eb  F   G   A   B
R  S  T  S  T   T   T   T
```

The degrees represent and identify the notes and their position inside the scale. Ordered in Roman numerals, the degrees of the Melodic Minor Scale are seven, starting from the first note (Root).

Referencing C Melodic Minor scale we find:

C = Root – I degree
D = 2nd – II degree
E♭ = ♭3rd – III degree
F = 4th – IV degree
G = 5th – V degree
A = 6th – VI degree
B = 7th – VII degree
C = 8ve – I degree

Each mode is associated with a grade of the Melodic Minor Scale and each one of them generates a type of chord or arpeggio related to its intervals (**Chord Tones**).
Chords and arpeggios are discussed in **Volume 2 – Arpeggios & Chords**.

Because each mode is basically a portion of the Melodic Minor Scale, they are seven combinations of the same *Scale Colour System* blocks applied to **The Melodic Minor Scale** – as seen in **The Minor Scales**.

The seven modes combined together provide all position combinations to play all the notes available in the specific key.

All of the following examples will be in C Melodic Minor – as it includes only one *flat* (♭). Once the Melodic Minor Scale and its Modes are learnt in one key, it will be easier to transpose them in all keys because of the transposing nature of the instrument. <u>Keys and transposition are discussed in **The Circle of Fifths** section</u>.

What follows is the list of the seven Melodic Minor Scale Modes with names, intervals and relative *Scale Colour System* code, followed by the Modes Chart diagrams – for both one finger per fret (**1Fpf**) and five frets per string stretched positions (**5fpS**).

I) **MELODIC MINOR** – Yellow, Red, Yellow

The Melodic Minor is the first of the Melodic Minor Modes. It features seven notes displaced at the specific distance **R T S T T T T S** and its intervals are:

Root
2nd = Major
♭3rd = Minor
4th = Perfect
5th = Perfect
6th = Major
7th = Major
8^{ve}

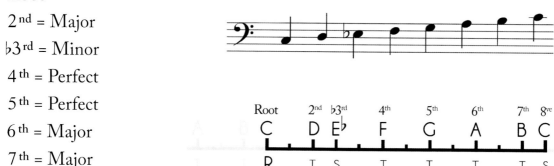

The **Root**, ♭3rd, 5th form a **Minor Triad** chord or arpeggio (C, E♭, G). Adding the 7th creates a **Minor Major7** chord or arpeggio (C, E♭, G, B).

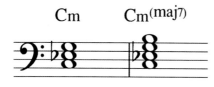

Colour code for **1Fpf** and **5fpS** positions. The dots represent the scale intervals.

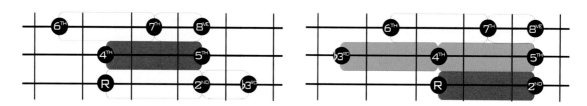

C Melodic Minor, **1Fpf** position, one octave – starting on C at fret *III* of the A string.

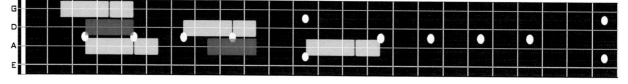

C Mel Minor, **5fpS** position on the entire fretboard – includes open strings A, D, G.

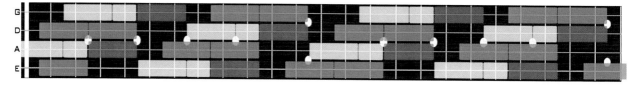

II) **DORIAN** ♭**2** – Blue, Red, Blue

The Dorian ♭2 is the second of the Melodic Minor Modes. It features seven notes displaced at the specific distance **R S T T T T S T** and its intervals are:

Root
♭2nd = Minor
♭3rd = Minor
4th = Perfect
5th = Perfect
6th = Major
♭7th = Minor
8ve

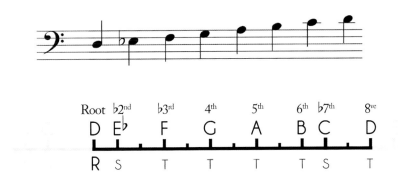

Root	♭2nd	♭3rd	4th	5th	6th	♭7th	8ve
D	E♭	F	G	A	B	C	D
R	S	T	T	T	T	S	T

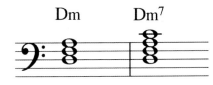

Dm   Dm⁷

The **Root**, ♭3rd, 5th of the Dorian mode form a **Minor Triad** chord or arpeggio (D, F, A). Adding the ♭7th creates a **Minor 7** chord or arpeggio (D, F, A, C).

Colour code for **1Fpf** and **5fpS*** positions. The dots represent the scale intervals.

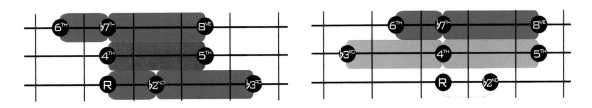

D Dorian ♭2, **1Fpf** position, one octave – starting on D at fret *V* of the A string.

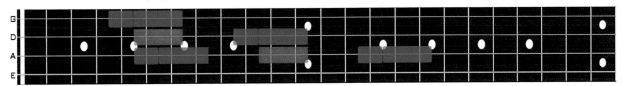

D Dorian ♭2, **1Fpf** position over the entire fretboard – includes open strings A, D, G.

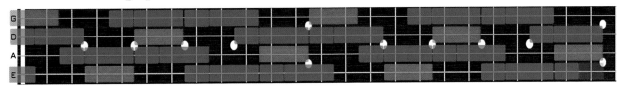

*5fpS positions are discussed in the **Colour Block Formula** at the end of this section.

III) **LYDIAN AUGMENTED** – Red, Green, Yellow

The Lydian Augmented (♯5) is the third of the Melodic Minor Modes. It features seven notes displaced at the specific distance **R T T T TS T S** and its intervals are:

Root

2 nd = Major

3 rd = Major

♯4 th = Augmented

♯5 th = Augmented

6 th = Major

7 th = Major

8 ve

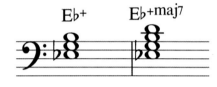

The **Root,** 3 rd, ♯5 th of the Lydian ♯5 mode form an **Augmented Triad** chord or arpeggio (E♭, G, B). Adding the 7 th creates an +Δ chord or arpeggio (E♭, G, B, D).

5fpS colour code positions. The dots represent the scale intervals.

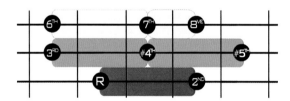

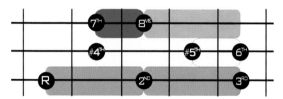

E♭ Lydian #5, **5fpS** position, one octave – starting on E♭ at fret *VI* of the A string.

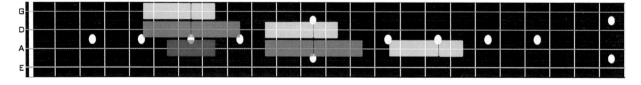

E♭ Lydian #5, **5fpS** position on the entire fretboard – includes open strings A, D, G.

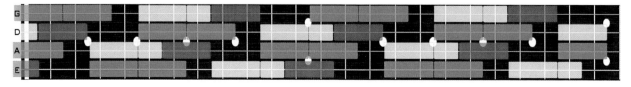

IV) **LYDIAN DOMINANT** – Red, Yellow, Blue

The Lydian Dominant is the fourth of the Melodic Minor Modes. It features seven notes displaced at the specific distance **R T T T S T S T** and its intervals are:

Root

2nd = Major

3rd = Major

♯4th = Augmented

5th = Perfect

6th = Major

♭7th = Minor

8^{ve}

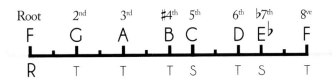

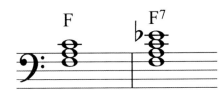

The **Root**, 3rd, 5th of the Lydian Dominant form a **Major Triad** chord or arpeggio (F, A, C). Adding the ♭7th creates a **7** chord or arpeggio (F, A, C, E♭).

Colour code for **1Fpf** and **5fpS*** positions. The dots represent the scale intervals.

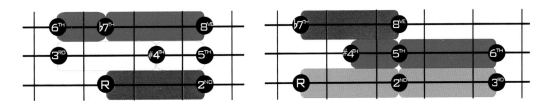

F Lydian Dominant, **1Fpf**, one octave – starting on F at fret V*III* of the A string.

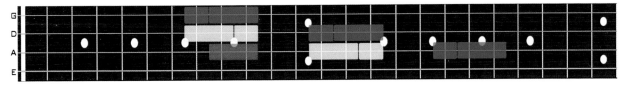

F Lydian Dominant, **1Fpf** on the entire fretboard – includes open strings A, D, G.

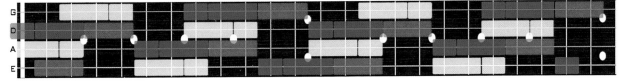

***5fpS** positions are discussed in the **Colour Block Formula** at the end of this section.

V) **MIXOLYDIAN** ♭**6** – Red, Blue, Green

The Mixolydian ♭6 is the fifth of the Melodic Minor Modes. It features seven notes displaced at the specific distance **R T T S T S T T** and its intervals are:

Root
2 nd = Major
3 rd = Major
4 th = Perfect
5 th = Perfect
♭6 th = Minor
♭7 th = Minor
8 ve

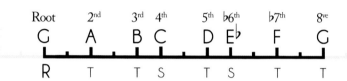

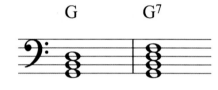

The **Root**, 3 rd, 5 th of the Mixolydian ♭6 mode form a **Major Triad** chord or arpeggio (G, B, D). Adding the ♭7 th creates a **7** chord or arpeggio (G, B, D, F).

5fpS colour code positions. The dots represent the scale intervals.

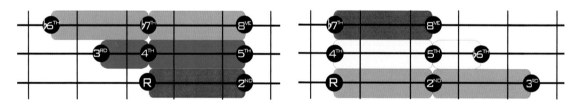

G Mixolydian ♭6, **5fpS** position, one octave – starting on G at fret *III* of the E string.

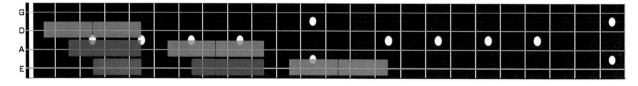

G Mixolydian ♭6, **5fpS** over the entire fretboard – includes open strings A, D, G.

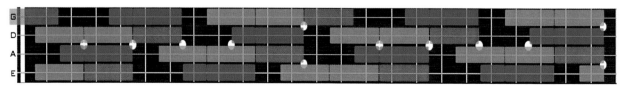

VI) **LOCRIAN** ♯**2** – Yellow, Blue, Red

The Locrian♯2 is the sixth of the Melodic Minor Modes. It features seven notes displaced at the specific distance **R T S T S T T T** and its intervals are:

Root

2nd = Major

♭3rd = Minor

4th = Perfect

♭5th = Diminished

♭6th = Minor

♭7th = Minor

8ve

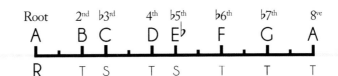

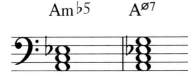

The **Root**, ♭3rd, ♭5th of the Locrian♯2 mode form a **Diminished Triad** chord/arpeggio (A, C, E♭). Adding the ♭7th creates a **Minor 7♭5 (ø)** chord/arpeggio (A, C, E♭, G).

Colour code for **1Fpf** and **5fpS*** positions. The dots represent the scale intervals.

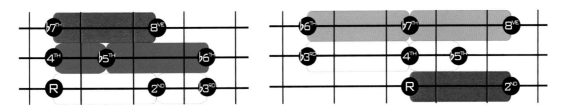

A Locrian ♯2, **1Fpf** position, one octave – starting on A at fret *V* of the E string.

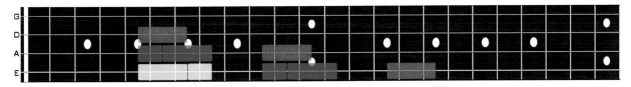

A Locrian ♯2, **1Fpf** position on the entire fretboard – includes open strings A, D, G.

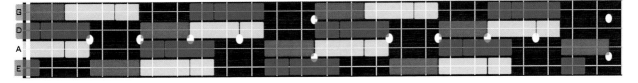

*5fpS positions are discussed in the **Colour Block Formula** at the end of this section.

49

VII) **ALTERED SCALE** – Blue, Green, Red

The Altered Scale is the seventh of the Melodic Minor Modes. It features seven notes displaced at the specific distance **R S T S T T T** and its intervals are:

Root
♭2nd = Minor
♭3rd = Minor
♭4th = Diminished
♭5th = Diminished
♭6th = Minor
♭7th = Minor
8ve

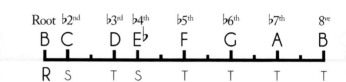

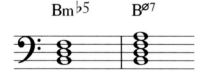

The **Root**, ♭3rd and ♭5th of the Altered Scale mode form a **Diminished Triad** chord/arpeggio (B, D, F). Adding the ♭7th creates a **Minor 7♭5 (ø)** chord or arpeggio (B, D, F, A).

5fpS colour code positions. The dots represent the scale intervals.

B Altered Scale, **5fpS** position, one octave– starting on B at fret *II* of the A string.

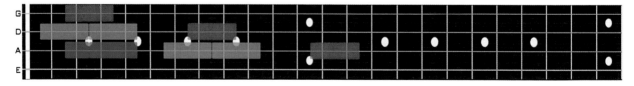

B Altered Scale **5fpS** position on the entire fretboard – includes open strings A, D, G.

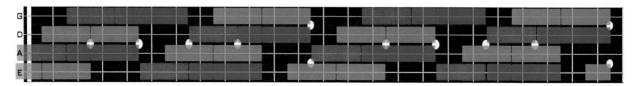

Melodic Minor Scale Colour Block Formulas

Because the Melodic Minor Scale has a fixed series of intervals, all colour block combinations follow two master colour block "formulas" – <u>starting from the V degree of the Melodic Minor Scale</u>, all Melodic Minor Modes positions are included in:

Red, Blue, Green, Yellow, Blue.

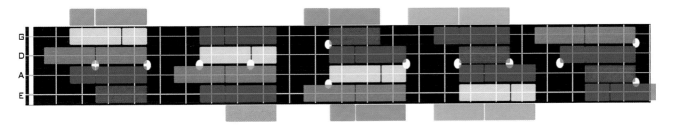

Green, Yellow, Green, Blue, Green, Yellow, Blue.

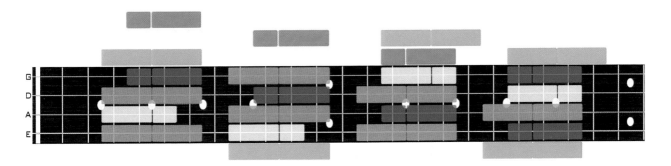

These two sequences are very useful to extend the scale of each Mode both vertically and horizontally on the neck – e.g. shifting position to play a two octave scale – and to visualise how Mode positions merge into each other's blocks.

> *i*
>
> Although the Melodic Minor Scale shares the same number of **Red**, **Blue**, **Yellow** and **Green** blocks of the Major Scale, their order and displacement changes.

Understanding how the scale patterns develop over the entire fretboard is vital for transposing scales in all keys, as the whole interval grid moves altogether – is notched down a string when moving keys up a fifth (C to G, D, A, E etc.), and one string up when moving down a fifth (C to F, B♭, E♭ etc.) – as showed in **The Circle of Fifths**.

C Melodic Minor Scale Modes

Melodic Minor Scale Modes: combinations of **Red**, **Blue**, **Yellow** and **Green** blocks.

I) C Melodic Minor

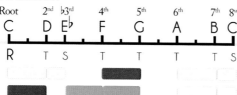

II) D Dorian ♭2

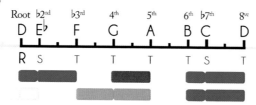

III) E♭ Lydian Augmented

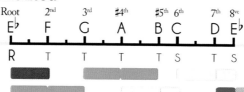

IV) F Lydian Dominant

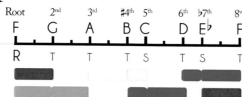

V) G Mixolydian ♭6

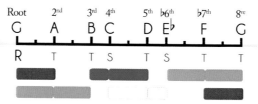

VI) A Locrian ♯2

VII) B Altered Scale

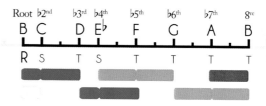

Melodic Minor Scale – Modes Chart

The numbered dots represent the suggested Fretting Hand fingering.

I) Melodic Minor

II) Dorian♭2

III) Lydian♯5

IV) Lydian Dominant

V) Mixolydian ♭6

VI) Locrian♯2

VII) Altered Scale

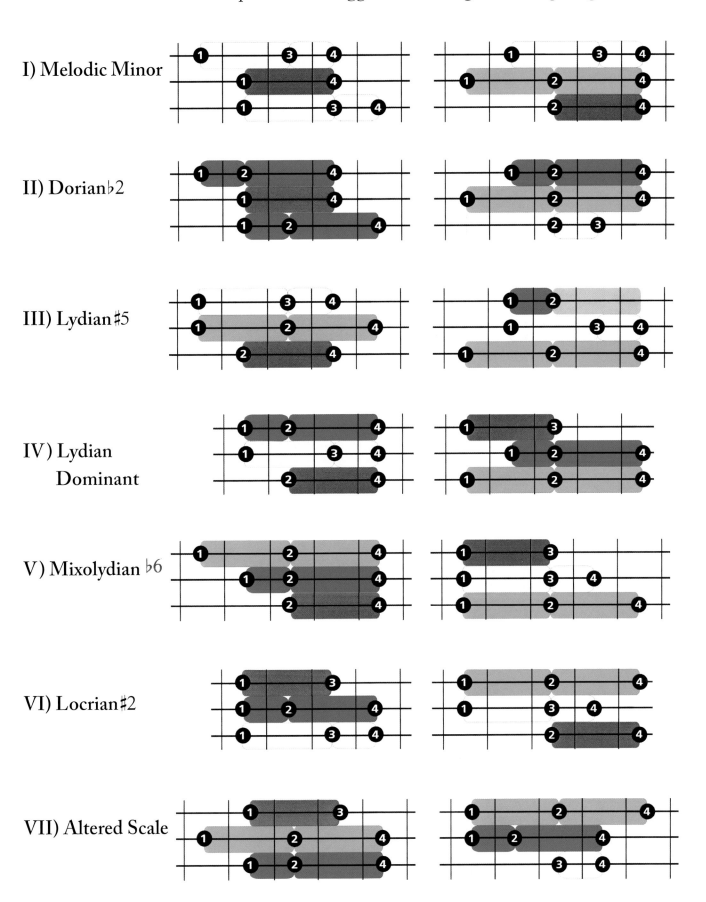

9. The Modes of the Harmonic Minor Scale

The Modes of the Harmonic Minor Scale are the seven interval permutations starting from each scale degree.

From each of the notes of the Harmonic Minor Scale we can build seven scales with different qualities and characteristics. These scales are called **Modes** and Mode I is the Harmonic Minor Scale. Because the note displacement changes depending on the note we start the scale from, each mode has a unique colour and interval structure.

As the Harmonic Minor Scale note sequence **R T S T T S $T_{1/2}$ S** repeats itself in each octave, we can identify seven permutations of this sequence starting from each degree of the scale.

I) Harmonic Minor

A	B C	D	E F		G♯ A
R	T S	T	T S		$T_{1/2}$ S

II) Locrian ♯6

B C	D	E F		G♯ A	B
R S	T	T S		$T_{1/2}$ S	T

III) Ionian ♯5

C	D	E F		G♯ A	B C
R	T	T S		$T_{1/2}$ S	T S

IV) Dorian ♯4

D	E F		G♯ A	B C	D
R	T S		$T_{1/2}$ S	T S	T

V) Phrygian Dominant

E F		G♯ A	B C	D	E
R S		$T_{1/2}$ S	T S	T	T

VI) Lydian ♯2

F		G♯ A	B C	D	E F
R		$T_{1/2}$ S	T S	T	T S

VII) Superlocrian

G♯ A	B C	D	E F		G♯
R S	T S	T	T S		$T_{1/2}$

The degrees represent and identify the notes and their position inside the scale. Ordered in Roman numerals, the degrees of the Harmonic Minor Scale are seven, starting from the first note (Root).

Referencing A Harmonic Minor scale we find:

A = Root – I degree

B = 2nd – II degree

C = ♭3rd – III degree

D = 4th – IV degree

E = 5th – V degree

F = ♭6th – VI degree

G♯ = 7th – VII degree

A = 8ve – I degree

Each mode is associated with a grade of the Harmonic Minor Scale and each one of them generates a type of chord or arpeggio related to its intervals (**Chord Tones**).
Chords and arpeggios are discussed in **Volume 2 – Arpeggios & Chords**.

Because each mode is basically a portion of the Harmonic Minor Scale, they are seven combinations of the same *Scale Colour System* blocks applied to **The Harmonic Minor Scale** – as seen in **The Minor Scales**.

The seven modes combined together provide all position combinations to play all the notes available in the specific key.

All of the following examples will be in A Harmonic Minor – as it includes only one *sharp* (♯). Once the Harmonic Minor Scale and its Modes are learnt in one key, it will be easier to transpose them in all keys because of the transposing nature of the instrument. <u>Keys and transposition are discussed in **The Circle of Fifths** section</u>.

What follows is the list of the seven Harmonic Minor Scale Modes with names, intervals and relative *Scale Colour System* code, followed by the Modes Chart diagrams – for both one finger per fret (**1Fpf**) and five frets per string stretched positions (**5fpS**).

I) **HARMONIC MINOR** – Red, Green, Orange

The Harmonic Minor scale is the first Modes. It features seven notes displaced at the specific distance **R T S T T S T T₁/₂ S** and its intervals are:

Root
2ⁿᵈ = Major
♭3ʳᵈ = Minor
4ᵗʰ = Perfect
5ᵗʰ = Perfect
♭6ᵗʰ = Minor
7ᵗʰ = Major
8ᵛᵉ

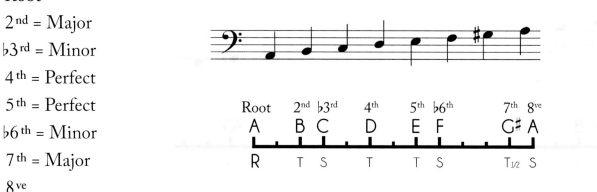

Am   Am(maj7)

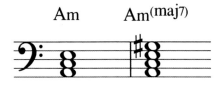

The **Root**, ♭3ʳᵈ, 5ᵗʰ form a **Minor Triad** chord or arpeggio (A, C, E). Adding the 7ᵗʰ creates a **Minor Major7** chord or arpeggio (A, C, E, G♯).

Colour code for **1Fpf** and **5fpS** positions. The dots represent the scale intervals.

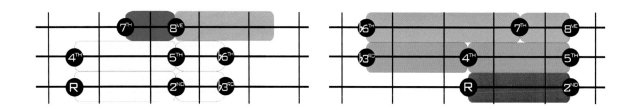

A Harmonic Min, **1Fpf** position, one octave – starting on A at fret *V* of the E string.

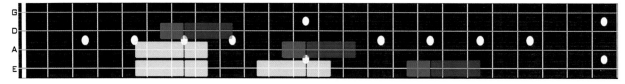

A Harmonic Minor, **5fpS** on the entire fretboard – includes open strings E, A, D.

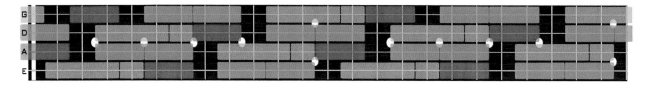

II) **LOCRIAN #6** – Blue, Purple, Red

The Locrian ♯6 is the second of the Harmonic Minor Modes. It features seven notes displaced at the specific distance **R S T T S T₁/₂ S T** and its intervals are:

Root
♭2ⁿᵈ = Minor
♭3ʳᵈ = Minor
4ᵗʰ = Perfect
♭5ᵗʰ = Diminished
6ᵗʰ = Major
♭7ᵗʰ = Minor
8ᵛᵉ

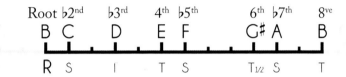

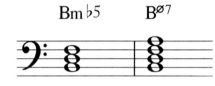

The **Root, ♭3ʳᵈ, ♭5ᵗʰ** of the Locrian ♯6 mode form a **Diminished Triad** chord/arpeggio (B, D, F). Adding the ♭7ᵗʰ creates a **Half Dim (ø7)** chord/arpeggio (B, D, F, A).

Colour code for **1Fpf** and **5fpS** positions. The dots represent the scale intervals.

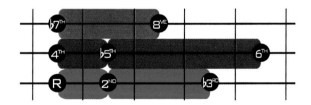

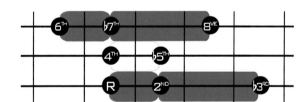

B Locrian ♯6, **5fpS** position, one octave – starting on B at fret *VII* of the E string.

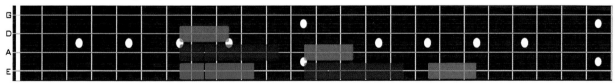

B Locrian ♯6, **5fpS** position over the entire fretboard – includes open strings E, A, D.

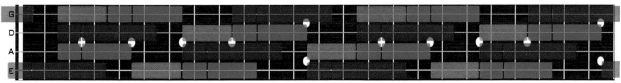

III) **IONIAN #5** – Red, Purple, Yellow

The Ionian ♯5 is the third of the Harmonic Minor Modes. It features seven notes displaced at the specific distance **R T T S T₁/₂ S T S** and its intervals are:

Root

2nd = Major

3rd = Major

4th = Perfect

♯5th = Augmented

6th = Major

7th = Major

8ve

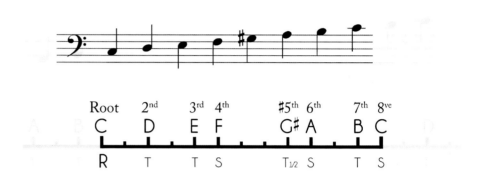

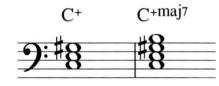

The **Root,** 3rd, ♯5th of the Ionian ♯5 mode form an **Augmented Triad** chord or arpeggio (C, E, G♯). Adding the 7th creates an +Δ chord or arpeggio (C, E, G♯, B).

Colour code for **5fpS** positions. The dots represent the scale intervals.

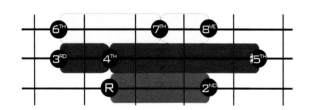
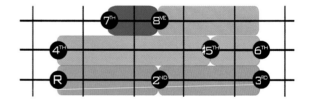

C Ionian ♯5, **5fpS** position, one octave – starting on C at fret *III* of the A string.

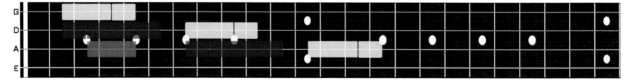

C Ionian ♯5, **5fpS** position on the entire fretboard – includes open strings E, A, D.

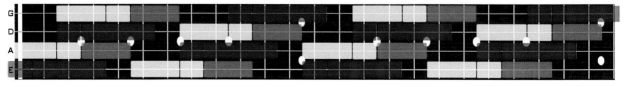

IV) **DORIAN #4** – Red, Orange, Blue

The Dorian♯4 is the fourth of the Harmonic Minor Modes. It features seven notes displaced at the specific distance **R T S T₁/₂ S T S T** and its intervals are:

Root

2nd = Major

♭3rd = Minor

♯4th = Augmented

5th = Perfect

6th = Major

♭7th = Minor

8ve

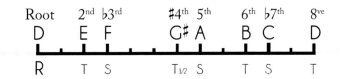

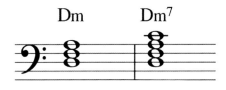

The **Root**, ♭3rd, 5th of the Dorian♯4 form a **Minor Triad** chord or arpeggio (D, F, A). Adding the ♭7th creates a **Minor 7** chord or arpeggio (D, F, A, C).

Colour code for **1Fpf** and **5fpS** positions. The dots represent the scale intervals.

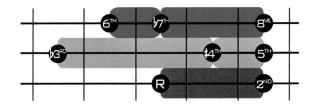

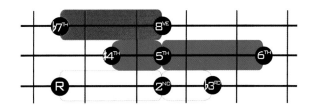

D Dorian ♯4, **5fpS** position, one octave – starting on D at fret *V* of the A string.

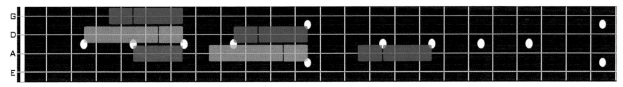

D Dorian ♯4, **5fpS** position over the entire fretboard – includes open strings E, A, D.

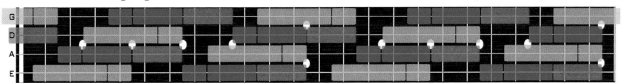

V) **PHRYGIAN DOMINANT** – Purple, Yellow, Red

The Phrygian Dominant is the fifth of the Harmonic Minor Modes. It features seven notes displaced at the distance **R S T$_{1/2}$ S T S T T**. Its intervals are:

Root

♭2nd = Minor

3rd = Major

4th = Perfect

5th = Perfect

♭6th = Minor

♭7th = Minor

8^{ve}

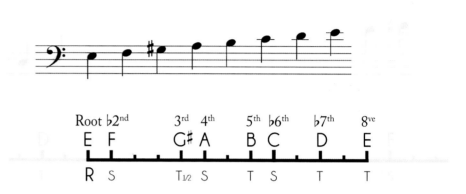

The **Root**, 3rd, 5th of the Phrygian Dominant mode form a **Major Triad** chord or arpeggio (E, G♯, B). Adding the ♭7th creates a **7** chord or arpeggio (E, G♯, B, D).

5fpS colour code positions. The dots represent the scale intervals.

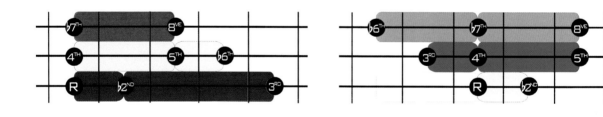

E Phrygian Dominant, **5fpS** position, one octave – starting at fret *VII* of the A string.

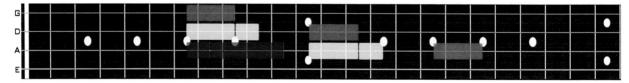

E Phrygian Dominant, **5fpS** over the entire fretboard – includes open strings E, A, D.

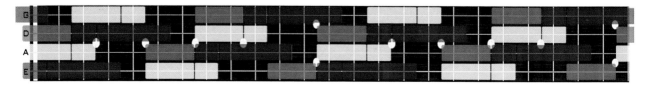

VI) **LYDIAN #2** – Orange, Blue, Purple

The Lydian #2 is the sixth of the Harmonic Minor Modes. It features seven notes displaced at the specific distance **R $T_{1/2}$ S T S T T S** and its intervals are:

Root

#2 nd = Augmented

3 rd = Major

#4 th = Augmented

5 th = Perfect

6 th = Major

7 th = Major

8 ve

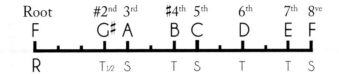

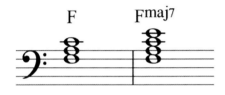

The **Root**, 3 rd, 5 th of the Lydian #2 mode form a **Major Triad** chord/arpeggio (F, A, C). Adding the 7 th creates a **Major 7** chord or arpeggio (F, A, C, E).

Colour code for **1Fpf** and **5fpS** positions. The dots represent the scale intervals.

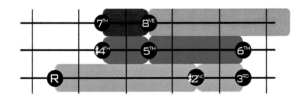

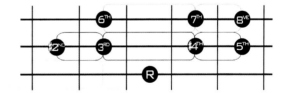

F Lydian #2, **5fpS** position, one octave – starting on F at fret *VIII* of the A string.

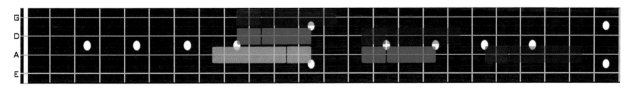

F Lydian #2, **5fpS** position on the entire fretboard – includes open strings E, A, D.

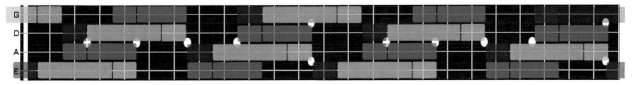

61

VII) **SUPERLOCRIAN** – Blue, Green, Orange

The Superlocrian is the seventh of the Harmonic Minor Modes. It features seven notes displaced at the specific distance R T T S T T S T$_{1/2}$ and its intervals are:

Root

b2nd = Minor

b3rd = Minor

b4th = Diminished

b5th = Diminished

b6th = Minor

bb7th = Diminished

8^{ve}

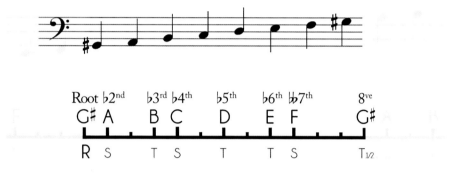

The **Root,** b3rd and b5th of the Superlocrian mode form a **Diminished Triad** chord/arpeggio (G♯, B, D). Adding the bb7th creates a **Diminished (o)** chord/arpeggio (G♯, B, D, F).

5fpS colour code positions. The dots represent the scale intervals.

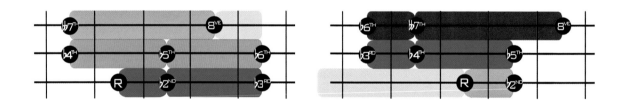

G♯ Superlocrian **5fpS** position, one octave – starting on G♯ at fret *IV* of the E string.

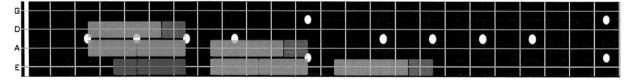

G♯ Superlocrian, **5fpS** on the entire fretboard – includes open strings E, A, D.

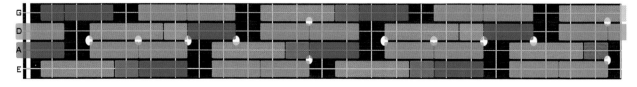

Harmonic Minor Scale Colour Block Formula

Because the Harmonic Minor Scale has a fixed series of intervals, all colour block combinations follow one master colour block "formula" – <u>starting from the VII degree of the Harmonic Minor Scale</u>, all Harmonic Minor Modes positions are included in:

Blue, Green, Orange, Blue, Purple, Yellow, Yellow.

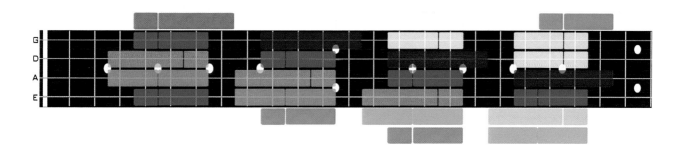

This sequence is very useful to extend the scale of each Mode both vertically and horizontally on the neck – e.g. shifting position to play a two octave scale – and to visualise how Mode positions merge into each other's blocks.

> *i* The two 'new' colour blocks introduced in the Harmonic Minor Scale are the **Orange** and **Purple**.
>
> They overlap the $T_{1/2}$ interval surrounded by two semitones featured in the scale sequence, as seen in Mode VI and Mode VII.
>
>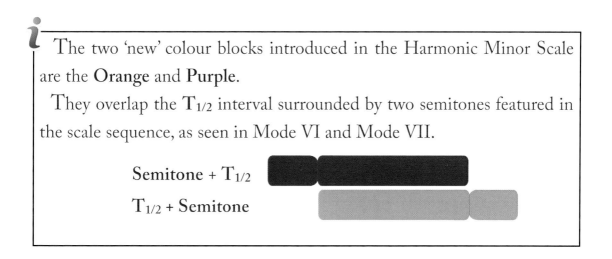
>
> Semitone + $T_{1/2}$
>
> $T_{1/2}$ + Semitone

Understanding how the scale patterns develop over the entire fretboard is vital for transposing scales in all keys, as the whole interval grid moves altogether – is notched down a string when moving keys up a fifth (C to G, D, A, E etc.), and one string up when moving down a fifth (C to F, B♭, E♭ etc.) – as showed in **The Circle of Fifths**.

A Harmonic Minor Scale Modes

Harmonic Minor Scale Modes: combinations of **Red**, **Blue**, **Yellow**, **Green** blocks.

I) A Harmonic Minor

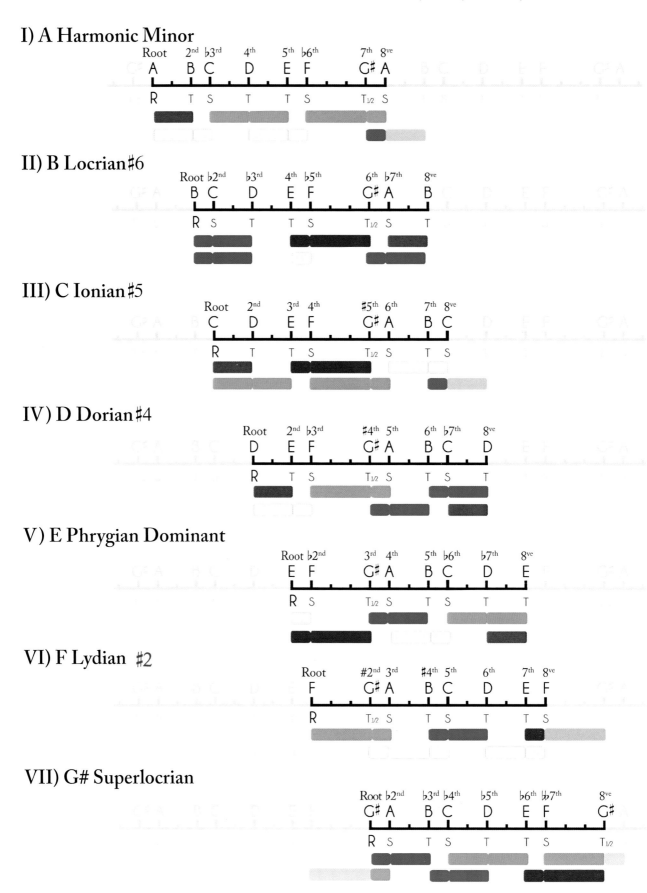

II) B Locrian♯6

III) C Ionian♯5

IV) D Dorian♯4

V) E Phrygian Dominant

VI) F Lydian ♯2

VII) G# Superlocrian

Harmonic Minor Scale – Modes Chart

The numbered dots represent the suggested Fretting Hand fingering.

I) Harmonic Minor

II) Locrian ♯6

III) Ionian ♯5

IV) Dorian ♯4

V) Phrygian Dominant

VI) Lydian ♯2

VII) Superlocrian

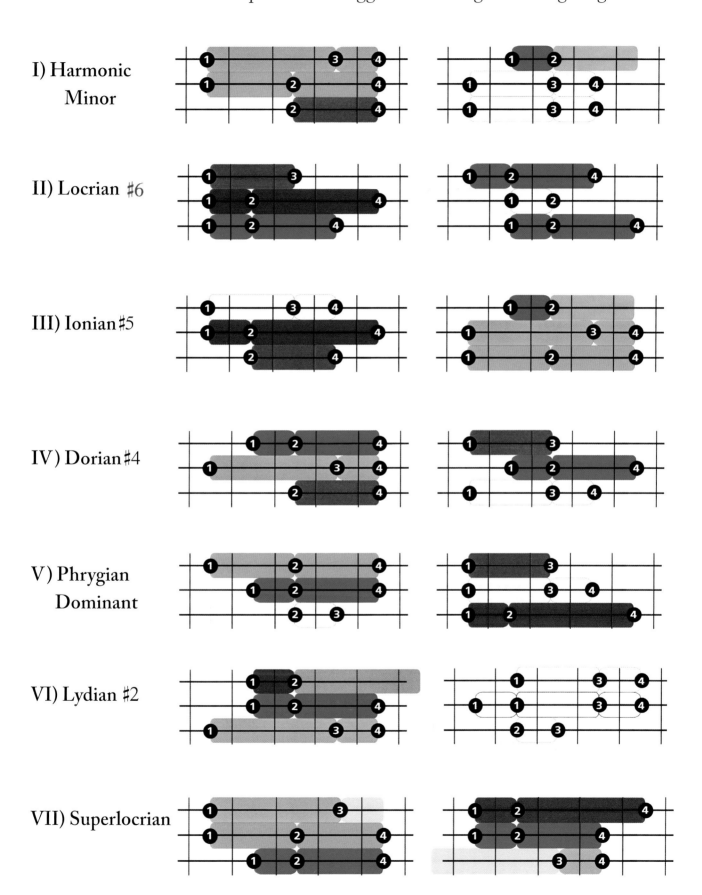

Heptatonic Scales Colour Block Formula

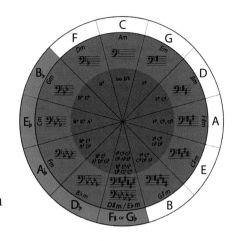

All the Heptatonic Scales, featuring seven note each, follow a similar interval pattern. As seen in each scale formula, each coloured block is stacked by fourths and starts on each of the seven scale degree.

To familiarise yourself with all of them I present an overview and comparative analysis of their structure.

The **Melodic Minor** and **Harmonic Minor** scales **differ by only one note** per octave from the *Diatonic* scales (Major Scale and Natural Minor Scale).

As the seven colour blocks Formula extends for three Octaves, three colour blocks of the Major Scale formula will be replaced in the Melodic and Harmonic Minor scales.

Major Scale, Natural Minor Scale (diatonic)	Melodic Minor Scale (non diatonic)	Harmonic Minor Scale (non diatonic)
Green	Green	*Blue
Green	*Yellow	Green
Green	Green	*Orange
Blue	Blue	Blue
Blue	*Green	*Purple
Yellow	Yellow	Yellow
Yellow	*Blue	Yellow

10. The Pentatonic Scale

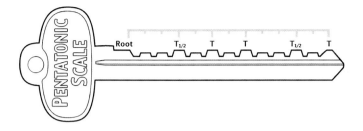

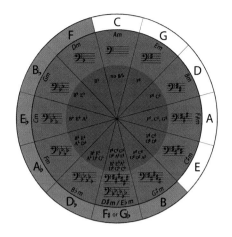

The Pentatonic Scale is undoubtedly the most popular scale in music. Still the subject of studies, the Pentatonic seems to be the only scale shared by all music culture across the world.

The name Pentatonic comes from the Greek word *Pénte* (πέντε) meaning five. Unsurprisingly the scale consists of a series of five notes.

The Pentatonic Scale is a very agile group of notes which completes one octave with just five sounds – as opposed to the seven of the Major Scale. It is widely used in all contemporary music styles (i.e. pop, rock, blues, jazz, funk) as well as folk and classic music.

Referencing the **The Circle of Fifths** diagram above, the notes of the Pentatonic Scale are five consecutive *fifths*. Therefore it is possible to obtain a Pentatonic Scale from any of the twelve notes in the *Circle of Fifths*.

The fives notes C, G, D, A, E around the *circle* correspond to A Pentatonic Scale.

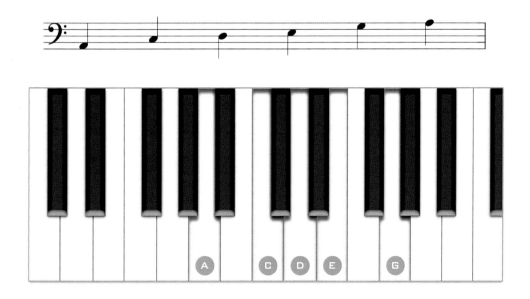

Minor Pentatonic or Major Pentatonic?

The Pentatonic is a minor scale featuring the **Root**, ♭3rd, **4th**, **5th** and ♭7th. It is used over *minor* and *minor 7* chords or arpeggios, and it is the most complete scale form amongst the five permutations built from each of the five notes of the Pentatonic Scale.

Unlike the Modes of the Major Scale however, the permutations of the Pentatonic Scale are called Positions, or **Shapes**, and they are related to the scale Root. This is because only five notes are not enough to generate five complete scales.

Interestingly though, the second shape of the Pentatonic scale corresponds to a *major* triad featuring the **2nd** and the **6th**. This Shape is used over *major* chords and arpeggios and it is often presented as Major Pentatonic scale.

The following examples and charts will refer to **A Pentatonic** (A, C, D, E, G).

Shape 1 – A Minor Pentatonic (A, C, D, E, G, A)

Shape 2 – C Major Pentatonic (C, D, E, G, A, C)

Shape 3 – (D, E, G, A, C, D)

Shape 4 – (E, G, A, C, D, E)

Shape 5 – (G, A, C, D, E, G)

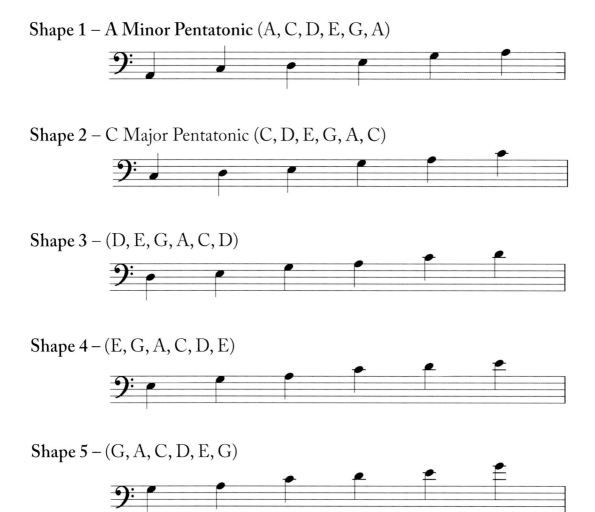

Pentatonic Scale Shapes

Starting from each of the five notes of the Pentatonic Scale it is possible to obtain the five Shapes of the scale.

As the five notes of the Pentatonic Scale are displaced at intervals of one Tone and one Tone and a half, they follow on the fretboard a two notes per string pattern (**2NpS**) with a One Finger per Fret position (**1Fpf**).

The *Scale Colour System* blocks for the intervals of the Pentatonic Scale are:

Tone (Red)

Tone and a Half (Grey*)

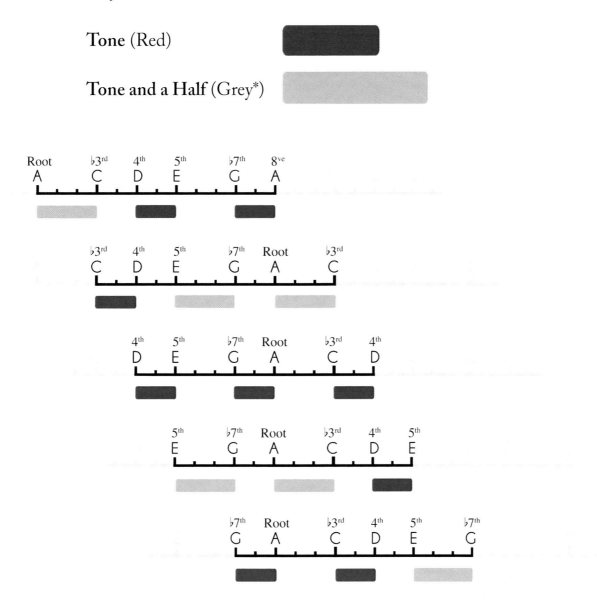

*The **Grey** block used for the 1.5 Tone interval references only the external notes of the block (digit 1-4).

All Shapes of the Pentatonic Scale line up on the fretboard in a conveniently symmetrical unit across three strings.

Note how Shapes 4 and 5 are flipped mirror images of shapes 1 and 2, divided by a central block (Shape 3).

Shape 1 – A Minor Pentatonic – Grey, Red, Red

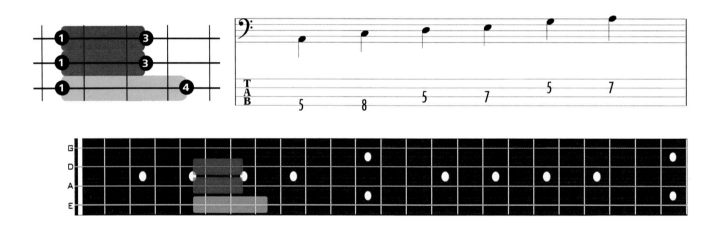

Shape 2 – C Major Pentatonic (staring from the ♭3ʳᵈ) – Red, Grey, Grey

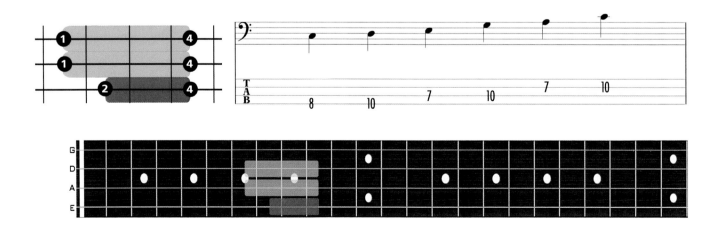

Shape 3 (starting from the 4th) – Red, Red, Red

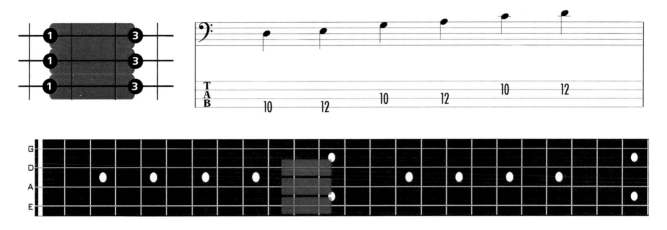

Shape 4 (starting from the 5th) – Grey, Grey, Red

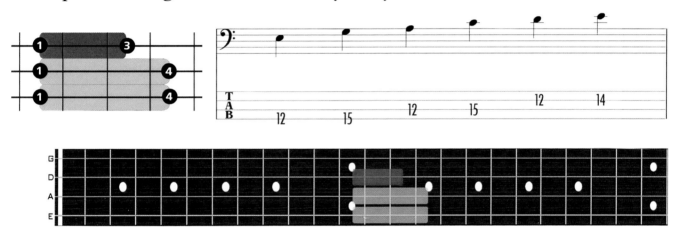

Shape 5 (starting from the ♭7th) – Red, Red, Grey

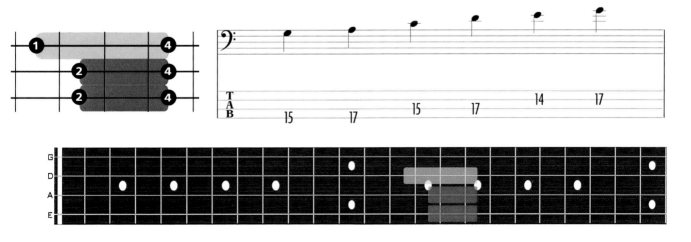

Pentatonic Scale Colour Block Formula

Because the Pentatonic Scale has a fixed series of intervals, the five block Shapes follow one master colour block "formula":

Grey, Grey, Red, Red, Red – <u>starting from the V degree of the Pentatonic Scale.</u>

Visualising this stacked sequence is very useful to extend the scale of each Shape vertically throughout the fretboard, and to visualise how all positions merge.

A Pentatonic Shapes **1Fpf** position extended for one octave across three strings.

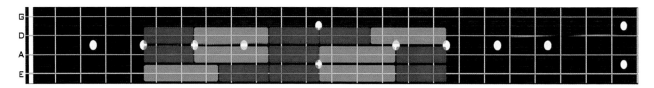

A Pentatonic **1Fpf** position on the entire fretboard – include open strings E, A, D, G.

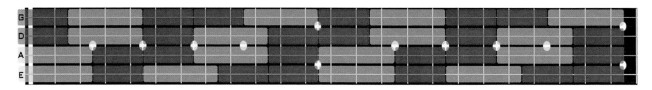

Understanding how the scale patterns develop over the entire fretboard is vital for transposing scales in all keys. The whole interval grid moves altogether – is notched down a string when moving keys up a fifth, and one string up when moving down a fifth – as showed in **The Circle of Fifths.**

Pentatonic Scale Shapes Chart

One octave scale – **1Fpf** blocks across three strings.
The numbered dot represent the suggested Fretting Hand fingering.

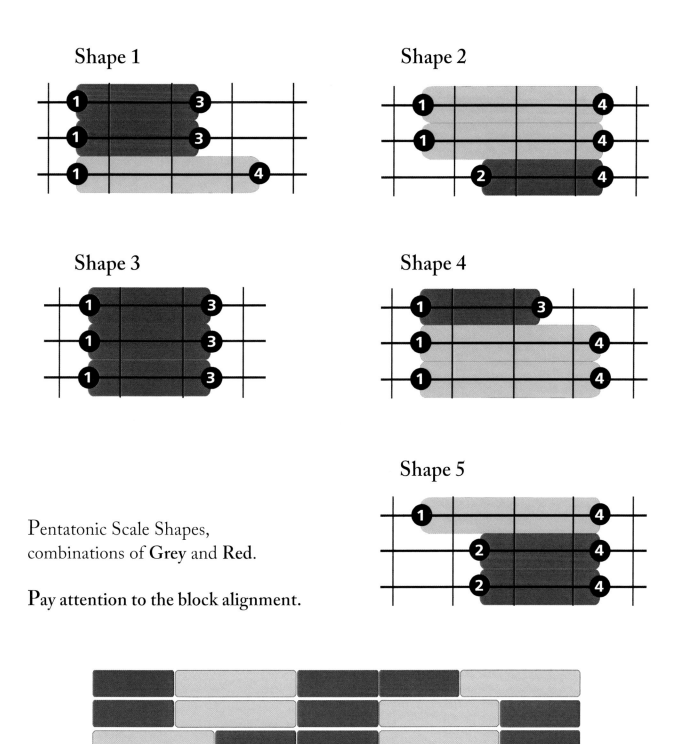

Pentatonic Scale Shapes,
combinations of **Grey** and **Red**.

Pay attention to the block alignment.

Two consecutive one Tone **Red** blocks can also be played as one **Green** block (**5fpS**).

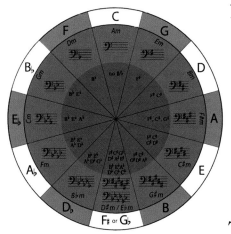

11. The Whole Tone Scale

Also called Symmetric, the Whole Tone scale consists of six notes displayed at one Tone interval from each other, dividing one Octave into six equal parts.

The Whole Tone Scale is a *Hexatonic* scale – from the Greek ἕξι (*éxi*), meaning six. Because of its symmetry, the Whole Tone scale has an undefined sound and, similarly to the Chromatic Scale, it takes its name from the starting note (**Root**). All twelve notes can be divided into two Whole Tone scale cycles.

Cycle 1

Root

2nd = Major

3rd = Major

♯4th = Augmented

♯5th = Augmented

♭7th = Minor

8^{ve}

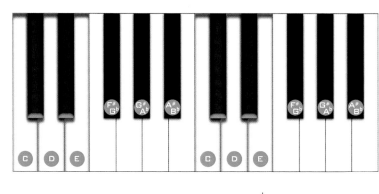

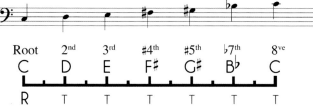

Cycle 2

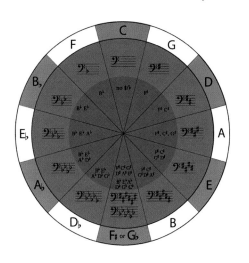

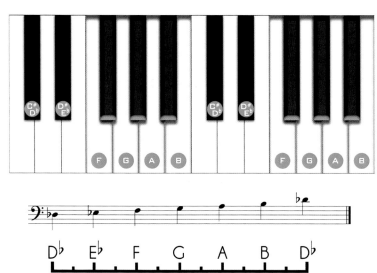

One Octave Whole Tone Scale – Red, Green, Red

The symmetry of the Whole Tone scale is clearly visible through its scale shape on the fretboard – since the six notes are displaced at one Tone distance from each other.

As all six notes are distributed at one tone interval **R T T T T T** it is possible to play this scale in a variety of digit combinations of two and three notes per string. The numbered dots represent the *Fretting Hand* fingering.

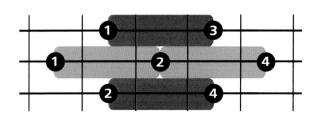

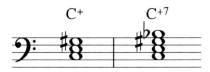

The **Root**, 3rd and $\sharp$5th of the Whole Tone Scale form an **Augmented Triad** chord or arpeggio (C, E, G$\sharp$). Adding the $\flat$7th creates a **Caug 7** chord/arpeggio (C, E, G$\sharp$, B$\flat$).

Example 1: C Whole Tone Scale, one octave in one position across three strings.

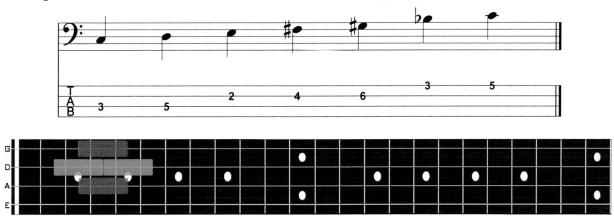

Note: the Whole Tone scale **Red** and **Green** blocks are <u>one Tone away from each other</u>.

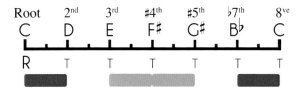

Two notes one Tone apart can either be two frets away on the same string (C-D); or three frets away on the adjacent string – covering a space of four frets **1Fpf** (D-E).

Each block can be shifted over the fretboard, to extend and displace the scale notes on any string and in any direction.

The symmetry of the fretboard allows you to find the same notes by shifting blocks horizontally.

Example 2: C Whole Tone Scale, one octave in two positions across two strings.

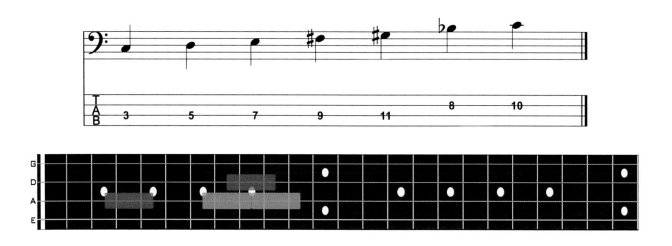

Displacing the notes on one string is a good way to learn the fretboard and familiarising oneself with all areas of the neck.

Example 3: C Whole Tone Scale, one octave in three positions across one string.

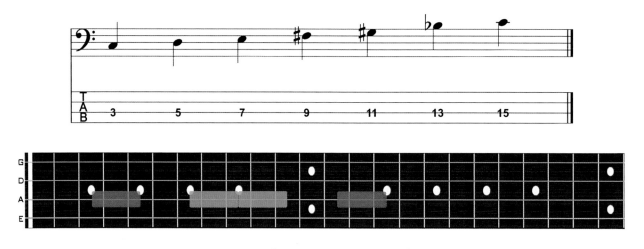

The displacement of all scale notes on the instrument will look clearer once all block structures are moved over the entire fretboard.

Stretched Position, Five frets per String (5fpS) – Green, Green, Green

Because the six notes of the Whole Tone scale are displaced symmetrically at one Tone distance, it is possible to play the scale diagonally over the fretboard using a two–Tones fingering combination (**Green** block).

This will involve a consistent Semitone shift when crossing each string and will allow to move fast across the fretboard.

Below are the two Whole Tone scale *cycles* starting from **C** and **D♭**.

Cycle 1

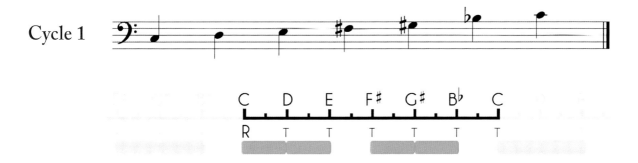

C Whole Tone Scale on the entire fretboard – include open strings E and D.

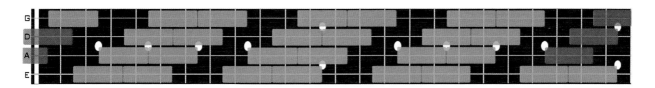

Cycle 2

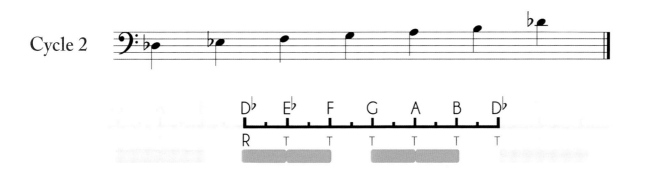

D♭ Whole Tone Scale on the entire fretboard – include open strings A and G.

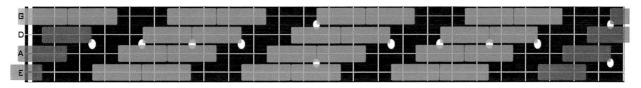

12. The Diminished Scales

*The Diminished scales feature eight notes displayed at alternating intervals of Semitone and Tone, creating two symmetric patterns: **Semitone-Tone** and **Tone-Semitone** scales.*

Also called *Octatonic* scales – from the Greek οκτώ (οκτό), meaning eight – the eight notes of the Diminished Scales can be seen as two *diminished arpeggios* starting on two notes either one Semitone or one Tone apart: i.e. C°, D♭° or C°, D°.

Semitone-Tone Scale

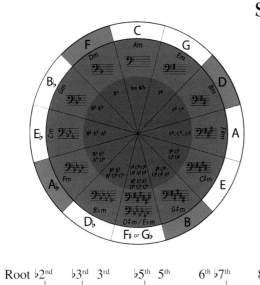

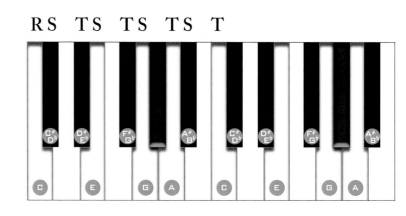

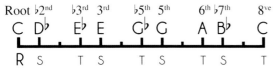

Tone–Semitone Scale

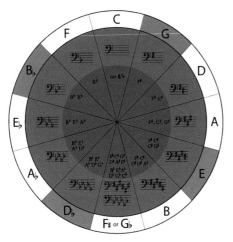

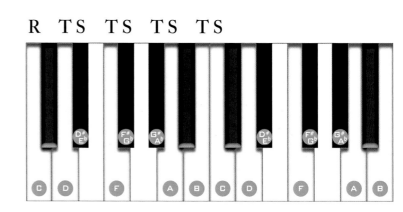

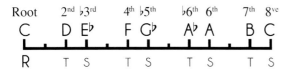

Semitone-Tone Scale – Blue, Yellow, Blue

The notes of the Semitone-Tone Scale (or *Half Step-Whole Step*) are distributed symmetrically at alternating intervals of Semitones and Tones: **R S T S T S T S T**.

This scale sequence corresponds to the notes of two Diminished Arpeggios positioned at one Semitone distance: i.e. **C°** and **D♭°** diminished arpeggios.

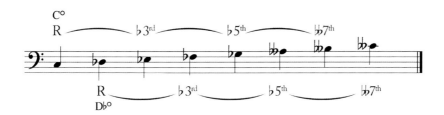

The equivalent *enharmonic* notes related to C are: **C, D♭, E♭, E, G♭, G, A, B♭, C.**

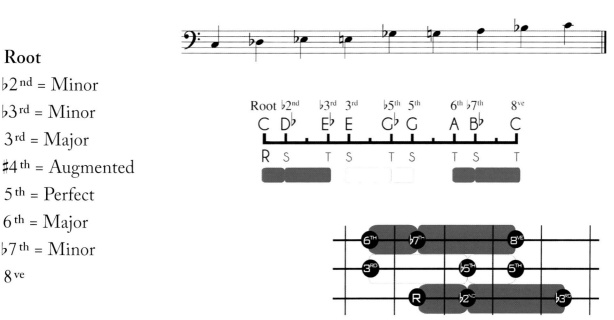

Root

♭2nd = Minor

♭3rd = Minor

3rd = Major

♯4th = Augmented

5th = Perfect

6th = Major

♭7th = Minor

8ve

As the Semitone-Tone Scale presents:

> **Major** and **Minor third** (♭3rd, 3rd),
> **Perfect** and **Diminished fifth** (♭5th is enharmonic of the ♯4th),
> **Minor** and **Diminished seventh** (♭♭7th is enharmonic to the Major 6th),
> **Minor** and **Augmented second** (♯2th is the enharmonic of ♭3th),

its notes can be combined to create a variety of chords and arpeggios.

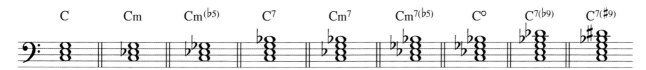

Due to the symmetrical displacement of the Semitone-Tone Scale notes it is possible to play them in a variety of digit combinations of three and four notes per string.

The numbered dots represent the *Fretting Hand* fingering for the three notes per string pattern (**3NpS**).

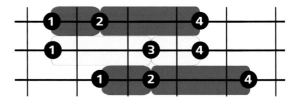

One octave Semitone-Tone Scale, starting on C at fret *III* on the A string.

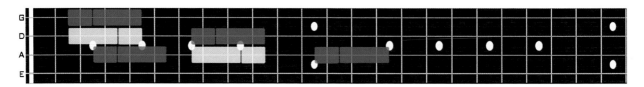

C Semitone-Tone Scale on the entire fretboard – include open strings E, A, G.

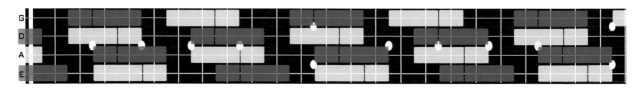

Note: the symmetry of the Diminished scales creates one unit of one **Yellow** and one **Blue** block stacked vertically (as they are one Tone from each other).
These **Yellow-Blue** unit are displaced at one Semitone distance from each other.

The same symmetry and colour pattern is also used for the other Diminished scale (Tone-Semitone) which, similarly to a Mode, simply starts on the other interval permutation of the scale.

Tone–Semitone Scale – Yellow, Blue, Yellow

The notes of the Tone-Semitone Scale (or *Whole Step-Half Step*) are distributed symmetrically at alternating intervals of Tones and Semitones: **R T S T S T S T S**.

This scale sequence corresponds to the notes of two Diminished Arpeggios positioned at one Tone distance: i.e. **C°** and **D°** diminished arpeggios.

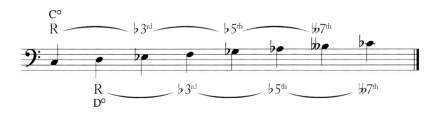

The equivalent *enharmonic* notes related to C are: **C, D, E♭, F, G♭, A♭, A, B, C.**

Root

2nd = Major

♭3rd = Minor

4th = Perfect

♭5th = Diminished

♭6th = Minor

6th = Major

7th = Major

8^{ve}

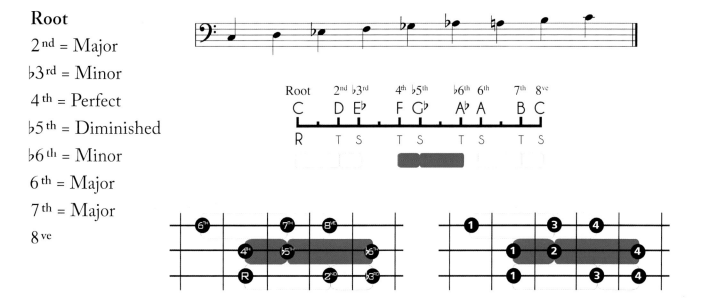

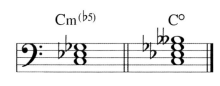

The **Root**, ♭3rd and ♭5th of the Tone-Semitone Scale form a **Diminished Triad** chord or arpeggio (C, E♭, G♭). Adding the ♭♭7th (enharmonic to the Major 6th) creates a **C Diminished** chord or arpeggio (**C°**).

One octave Semitone-Tone Scale, starting on C at fret *III* on the A string.

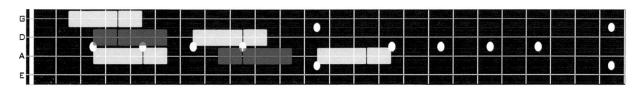

C Semitone-Tone Scale on the entire fretboard – include open strings A and D.

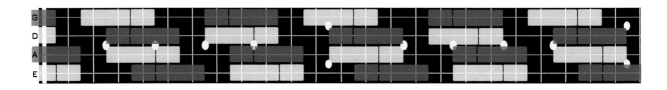

Four Notes per String – Semitone, Tone, Semitone

An alternative F.H. fingering is available to play four notes per string patterns (**4NpS**) and cover a **Semitone-Tone-Semitone** block (**STS**) joining together the **Blue** and **Yellow** blocks.

Semitone + Tone (Blue)
Semitone + Tone + Semitone (White)
Tone + Semitone (Yellow)

You can slide either finger .1 or .4 to to switch between the Blue and Yellow blocks when ascending or descending.

C **Semitone-Tone** scale over the entire fretboard. Include the open strings E, A, G.

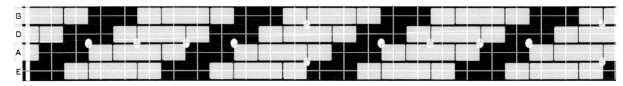

C **Tone-Semitone** scale over the entire fretboard. Include the open strings A and D.

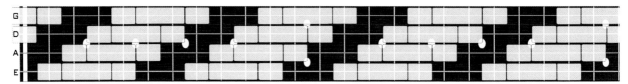

Note: the **STS** blocks are at one Tone distance between each other and shift by one Semitone per ascending string.

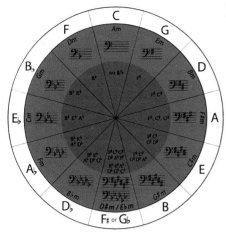

13. The Chromatic Scale

The Chromatic Scale is a symmetrical scale made of twelve equidistant notes.

The series of all twelve notes available in the Western music system is called the Chromatic Scale. All the notes are displaced at the distance of one Semitone, or *Half Step*, dividing one Octave into twelve equal parts.

As the Chromatic Scale <u>includes all notes</u>, generally it takes the name from the starting note (Root). The same note sequence repeats symmetrically at any octave.

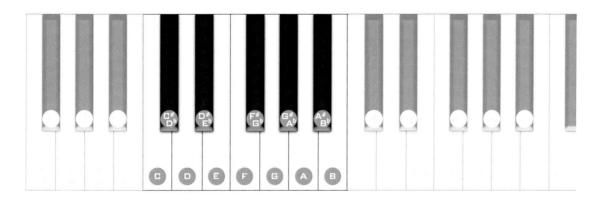

It is common to present the Chromatic scale starting from note C, extended for one octave. It includes all available twelve notes and they are named:

C C♯ D D♯ E F F♯ G G♯ A A♯ B (C) – when ascending;

C B B♭ A A♭ G G♭ F E E♭ D D♭ (C) – when descending.

The different use of the *enharmonic* notes in the ascending and descending sequence is due to the convention adopted in music: notes become *sharp* when moving up (♯), and *flat* when moving down (♭). As *accidentals* raise or lower notes by one Semitone, they are used to indicate the direction of the notes to simplify reading.

Four Notes per String Block (4NpS)

The following examples are the four most useful positions to play the 12 Chromatic scale notes extended for one octave over the fretboard.

Example 1: Chromatic Scale and hand blocks.

By employing the F.H. as a *four notes per string* block (**4NpS**) spaced at one finger per fret (**1Fpf**), the 12 notes within of the Chromatic Scale require three hand position shifts over one string.

i.e. 3 x 4NpS = 12 Notes

The brackets indicate the **4NpS** blocks and relative F.H. digit.

The **White** block on the fretboard represent the area covered by the four F.H. fingers.

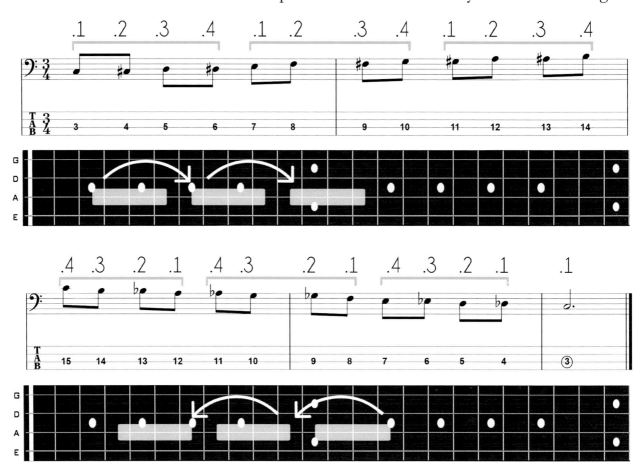

Note: To keep the **4NpS** block consistent when ascending or descending slide fingers .4 and .1 to reach the Octave/Root. When descending move the whole F.H. at once as a block spaced at one finger per fret.

Example 2: Chromatic Scale across three strings.

The second way to play the Chromatic scale is by moving two **4NpS** blocks across three strings. Notes are displaced in a more contained area of the fretboard involving smaller jumps – just one Semitone shift is involved when crossing one string.

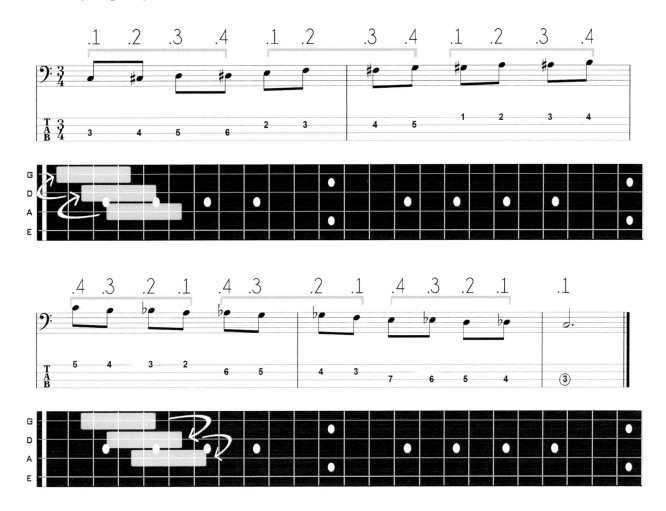

Note: The three hand blocks shift consistently one semitone up when descending – as finger .4 slides up one Semitone to reach the Octave at fret *V* on the G. Similarly, finger .1 slides one Semitone down to reach the Root.

When crossing the string using **4NpS** blocks there is a counterintuitive hand shift opposite to the direction: one Semitone down when ascending; one Semitone up when descending.

Stretched Position Across Three Strings

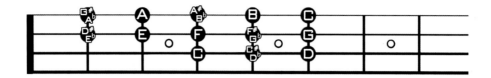

This position <u>allows you to access all notes without moving the Fretting Hand at all</u>. Finger .1 stretches one Semitone covering a five-fret space over one string (**5fpS**), and slides up to play two consecutive notes.

Example 3:

The scale will now start with finger .2.

Finger .1 stretches one Semitone to reach **D♯/E♭** and **G♯/A♭** notes.

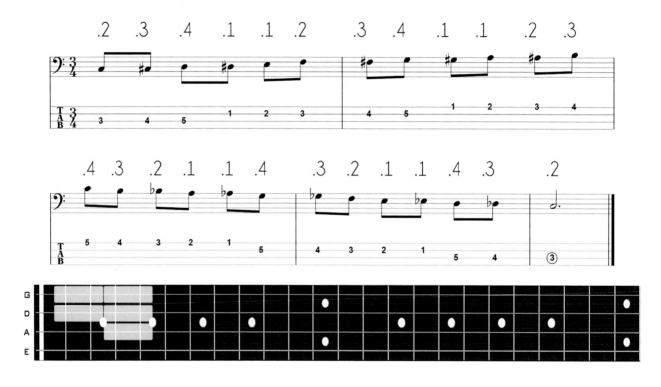

Note: When stretching finger .1 <u>keep the other fingers on their allocated frets</u> so that the hand block position remains consistent.

<u>THIS POSITION CONTAINS ALL SCALE SHAPES</u>.

Because no hand shifts or open strings are involved in this shape, it can be easily transposed anywhere over the fretboard starting on any note.

Example 3.1 – Stretched Position across three strings

Frets in the lower register of the neck are pretty wide and stretching can be very hard at first. To practice more comfortably and to explore the upper area of the neck, play the stretched position starting from C at fret *VIII* on the E string.

The One Octave Chromatic Scale vertical position is more suitable for skipping notes and contains the shapes of all existing scales.

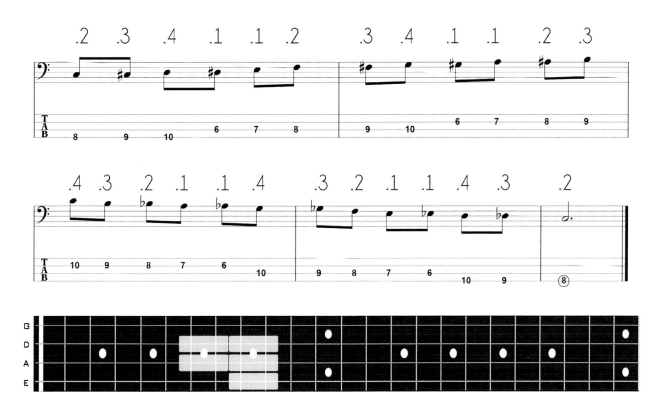

Note: To practice the stretch keep the F.H. fingers in position **1Fpf** and try to extend only finger .1 while keeping fingers .2, .3 and .4 on their allocated fret. If the stretch is too large practice this position starting on fret *VIII* on the E string.

Example 4: Open Strings Position

Practicing everything in first position using the open strings is an excellent way to acquire a complete understanding of the geometry of the neck.

Here is one octave C Chromatic Scale using the **Open Strings**:

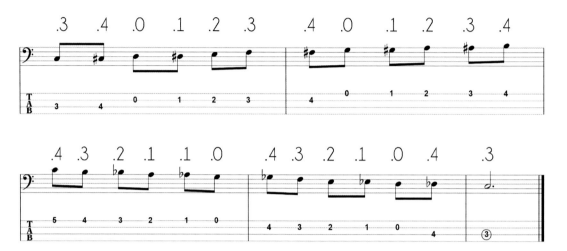

Note: It will require more accuracy and control of both Fretting and Picking hands to mute the open strings and avoid unwanted resonances. The Open Strings are extremely useful also when playing fretless instruments – as open strings do not need to be intonated.

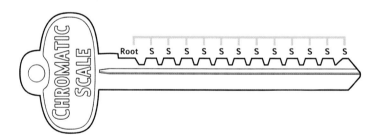

I do encourage you to explore other possible digit combinations available once you are comfortable and familiar with the four positions above and you have learned the notes on the fretboard.

You then can start mixing up the position and moving around the neck i.e. ascending with one position and descending with another one. Knowing the notes on the instrument is crucial and it allows you to target notes and decide the most convenient fretting hand fingering to adopt.

RECAP

USE THE CHROMATIC SCALE TO LEARN THE NOTES ON THE FRETBOARD.

There are only twelve notes to learn so it should not take too long to memorise their name and position over the fretboard once they are organised in convenient 4 note blocks.

Practice the Chromatic Scale to strengthen your *Fretting Hand* and use it as a geographical locator for every note. Keep the **4NpS** blocks spacing one finger per fret (**1Fpf**).

To learn the fretboard start to identify the *natural* **notes inside each block** – both ascending and descending on one string (**Example 1**). The very same blocks (and the notes they comprise) can be moved across the strings as showed in **Example 2**.

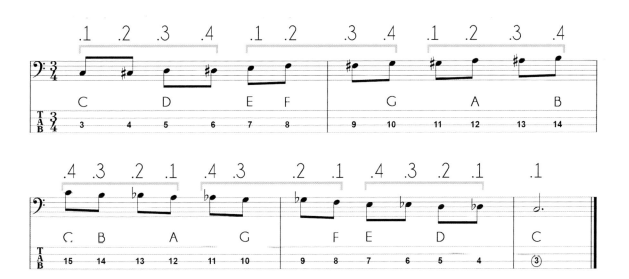

For a visual reference on your instrument you can use the dot markers – either on the fretboard or on its side. They mark the odd number frets: *III, V, VII, IX*. The double dot marks the octave above the open string – fret *XII*. Above fret *XII* the notes repeat in the exact same way as from the *nut* (fret *0*).

i The **Chromatic Scale contains all notes available in the Western Music System** – meaning that any scale, chord or arpeggio, is created by combining a selection of the notes included in the Chromatic Scale.

While **Chords** and **Arpeggios** are combinations of three or more notes stacked in thirds – *Triads*, *Seventh Chords*, and the extensions (*ninth*, *eleven* and *thirteen*) – **Scales** are sequences of adjacent intervals:

5 notes – **Pentatonic Scale**
6 notes – **Whole Tone Scale** (Symmetric)
7 notes – **Major** and **Minor Scales** (Heptatonic)
8 notes – **Semitone-Whole Tone** and **Whole Tone-Semitone** scales (Symmetrical)
12 notes in the **Chromatic Scale** (Symmetrical)

I believe it is vital to learn the Chromatic Scale to understand how all notes are displaced on the instrument. Explore all areas of the neck to learn how to play them over the entire fretboard and to acquire the dexterity to master the instrument.

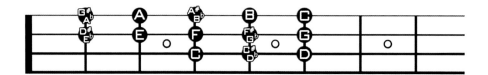

Seven notes are *Natural*, five are *Enharmonic*.
There are only 12 notes to remember after all.

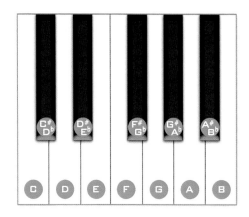

Colour Block Key

The Colour Blocks represent all the interval combinations found in music scales – divided into patterns of Two, Three and Four notes per string.

Refer to the Scale Charts for the suggested Fretting Hand digit*.

Two Notes per String (2NpS)

Tone (Red)

$T_{1/2}$ (Grey)

Three Notes per String (3NpS)

Semitone + Tone (Blue)

Tone + Semitone (Yellow)

Tone + Tone (Green)

$T_{1/2}$ + Semitone (Orange)

Semitone + $T_{1/2}$ (Purple)

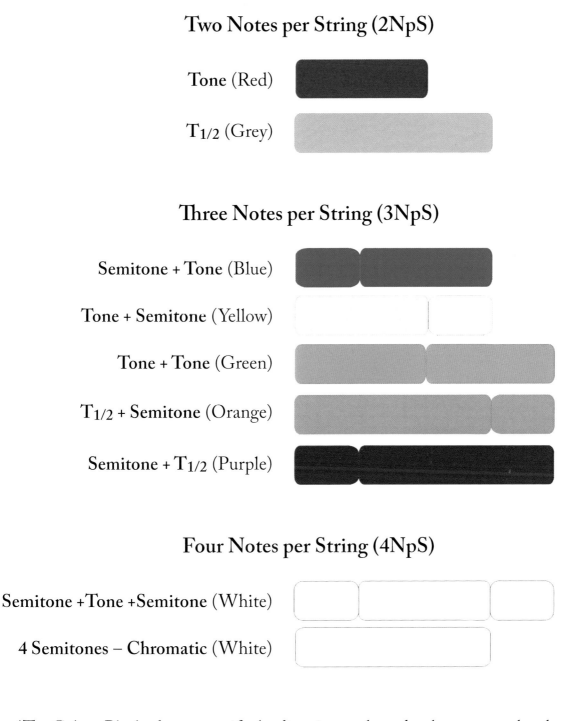

Four Notes per String (4NpS)

Semitone +Tone +Semitone (White)

4 Semitones – Chromatic (White)

*The Colour Blocks do not specify the direction or the order the notes can be played in.

Glossary

Accidental: Temporary alteration: *Sharp* (♯), *Flat* (♭), *Natural* (♮). Accidentals override the alterations in the *Key Signature* only for the duration of the bar they are used in. Unless indicated otherwise, *Accidentals* will not affect the notes in the following bars.

Alteration: Indicates whether a note is *sharp* (♯) or *flat* (♭). The *natural* sign (♮) reverts the note to its unaltered *natural* pitch.
(see *Natural Note*)

Arpeggio: Also called *Broken Chord*, an *Arpeggio* corresponds to the succession of notes forming a Chord.

Augmented: The ♯4th, ♯5th, ♯2nd intervals are called *Augmented*, indicating that they are raised by a *Semitone* from the position set by the Major Scale. *Augmented Triads* feature the **Root**, 3rd and ♯5th.

Circle of Fifths: The sequence of twelve notes used in Western music ordered by intervals of consecutive Fifths. After twelve consecutive fifths, the cycle ends on the starting note. The *Circle of Fifths* also represents the *Keys* ordered by number of *alterations*.

Chord: Three or more notes played simultaneously. Built by stacking notes in thirds (e.g. **Root**, 3rd, 5th, 7th, 9th, 11th, 13th), Chords create the Harmony. Two notes played simultaneously are called *Double Stops*.

Chord Tone/s: The note/s forming a Chord.

Chromatic: Proceeding by Semitones. The *Chromatic Scale* is the sequence of twelve notes displayed at the consecutive interval of one Semitone.

Diatonic: Indicates that the scale includes two Semitone intervals divided by either two or three consecutive Tone intervals. The Major Scale and its Modes are *Diatonic* scales.

Diminished: The ♭4th, ♭5th and ♭♭7th intervals are called *Diminished*.
Diminished Triads feature the **Root**, ♭3rd, ♭5th.
Diminished Seventh chords feature the **Root**, ♭3rd, ♭5th, ♭♭7th.

Enharmonic: Notes corresponding to the same pitch but are named differently depending on their intervallic and harmonic function.

Equal Temperament: The symmetrical tuning system adopted in Western music. It revolves around the interval of a fifth (pure fifth ratio = 3:2) which has been narrowed and adjusted so that any note can be found after a cycle of twelve consecutive fifths (see also *Circle of Fifths*).
Due to this tuning arrangement one *Octave* is divided into twelve equidistant notes separated by the interval of one *Semitone*.
The standard reference pitch for this system is centred around the frequency of 440 Hz corresponding to the note A_4.

Flat (♭): Indicates that the note is lowered by one Semitone.
Also used to describe interval qualities (♭2nd, ♭3rd, ♭4th, ♭5th, ♭6th, ♭7th) indicates they are lowered by a *Semitone* from the position set by the Major Scale.
Double Flat (♭♭) lowers a note by one Tone.

Heptatonic: Scale made up of seven notes. The Major Scale, Natural Minor Scale, Melodic Minor and Harmonic Minor Scale are *Heptatonic* scales.

Hexatonic: Scale made up of six notes. The Whole Tone Scale is a *Hexatonic* scale.

Interval:	The distance between two notes. Described in Tones or Semitones it represents the relationship between a starting note (Root) and its *interval*. The *Interval Sequence* is the sequence of the distances at which each scale note is displayed in relation to the scale Root.
Major:	Referring to intervals (2nd, 3rd, 6th, 7th) it indicates the quality and specific distance in relation to a starting note (Root). Referring to the *Tonality* it indicates that a piece of music uses the notes of the Major Scale.
Major Scale:	Made up of seven notes, the Major Scale is the model scale around which notes in Western music are organised. Its interval sequence **R T T S T T T S** is the blueprint for all major scales.
Melody:	The Melody is the succession of notes over time.
Minor:	Referring to intervals (2nd, 3rd, 6th, 7th) indicates the quality and specific distance in relation to a starting note (Root). Referring to the *Tonality* it indicates that a piece of music revolves around a Minor Scale.
Mode/s:	The interval permutation of a seven note scale (*Heptatonic*). By starting the interval series from each scale degree there are seven combinations (permutations) of intervals. The *Pentatonic* and *Symmetrical Scales* do not generate *Modes*.
Natural (♮):	Used to disable any alteration (♯ or ♭), it indicates that the targeted note is reverted to its *natural* state.
Natural Note:	The *Natural* notes are seven C, D, E, F, G, A, B. The sequence of the seven *natural* notes starting from the note C is called the **C Major Scale**. The nomenclature and interval relationship between notes in Western music is based around this major scale and it serves as model scale. It is a convention.

Octatonic: Scale made up of eight notes. The Diminished Scales (Semitone-Tone and Tone-Semitone) are *Octatonic Scales*.

Octave: The frequency ratio of two notes one octave apart is 2:1.
The frequency of one octave is exactly double the frequency of the Root; the octave below the Root vibrates at half the frequency.
Octaves define the degree of 'highness' or 'lowness' of notes corresponding to the same pitch class and have the same letter name.
In the Equal Temperament system the interval of one Octave is divided into twelve equal parts – twelve equidistant *Semitones*.

Pentatonic: Scale made up of five notes.

Perfect: Refers to the quality of the interval (4th, 5th) indicating the specific distance relative to the Root. A *Perfect* 4th is at 2.5 Tone from the Root; a *Perfect* 5th is at 3.5 Tones from the Root.

Root: The Root or Tonic is the reference note and starting point from which scale and chord intervals are related to.

Scale: Musical scales are organised sequence of notes, ordered by pitch, and positioned at specific distances – called intervals – in relation to the starting note, the Root. The sound and the name of scales are determined by the notes they comprise and, although they may differ in the number of notes (5 to 12), the structure of each scale repeats identically at any *Octave*.

Semitone (S):   The smallest interval between two notes, it corresponds to one fret space on the fretboard or one key space on the piano keyboard. The interval of one *Octave* is divided into twelve equidistant Semitones.

Sharp (♯):   Indicates that the note is raised by one *Semitone*. Also used to describe interval qualities (♯2nd,♯3rd, ♯4th,♯5th, ♯6th, ♯7th).
Double Sharp (𝄪) raises a note by one Tone.

Tonality: *Major* or *Minor*, it describes the character or mood of a piece of music. Usually the Major tonality is *bright* and *cheerful*, and the Minor is *darker* and more *contemplative*.

The tonality refers to the Major or Minor scale notes – meaning that the notes and the chord sequence revolve and are built following the intervals of either type of scale.

Tone (T):   Also called a *Whole Step*, a Tone is the interval of two *Semitones* between two notes - it corresponds to the distance of two frets.

Transpose: To move a set of notes up or down in pitch keeping the intervals between each note constant.

Triad: The **Root**, 3rd and 5th note of a scale form a Triad. They can be played simultaneously (chord) or in a sequence (arpeggio). Triads are the basic unit of harmony.

The quality of the 3rd and the 5th determine the type of triad (*major*, *minor*, *augmented* or *diminished*).

Unison: The interval of 0 *Semitone* between two notes is called Unison, corresponding to the same pitch. Also two note at different octaves are called a Unison - since the same note but at different register.

Bibliography

Campagnoli, B. (1797?). [facsimile] *Nuovo Metodo della Meccanica Progressiva*. Parallel Italian/French edition. Florence: Ricordi (1815?).

Duffin, R. W. (2008). *How Equal Temperament Ruined Harmony – and why you should care.* New York: W. W. Norton.

Ellis, A. J. (1885). *On The Musical Scales of Various Nations.* Journal of the Society of Arts 33. pp 485-527.

Holdsworth, A. (1992). *Allan Holdsworth.* 74 mins. Usa: Alfred Music Publishing Co. [Video:DVD].

La Motte, D. (1992). *Manuale di Armonia.* Perugia: La Nuova Italia Editrice.

Pastorius, J. (2002). *Modern Electric Bass*, 85 mins. Usa: Alfred Music Publishing Co. [Video:DVD].

Patel, A. D. (2010). *Music, Language, and the Brain.* New York: Oxford University Press.

Prelleur, P. (1731). [facsimile]. *The Modern Musick-Master, or The Universal Musician.* London: The Printing Office.

Renold, M. (2004). *Intervals, Scales, Tones and the concert pitch C = 128Hz.* Forest Row: Temple Lodge Publishing.

Schenker, H. (1954). *Harmony.* Boston: The University of Chicago Press.

Schoenberg, A. (1978). *Theory Of Harmony.* Los Angeles: University of California Press.

Segovia, A. (1953). *Diatonic Major and Minor Scales.* Washington D.C.: Columbia Music.

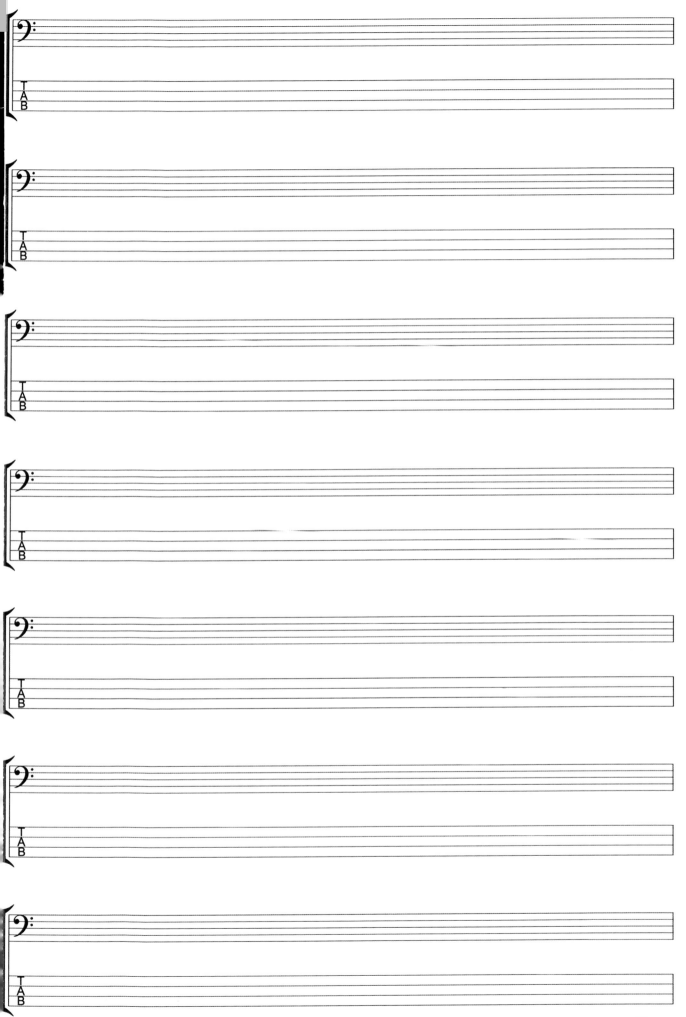

Blank Fretboard – Bass (20 Frets)

Print out and draw your *Scale Colour System* maps.

Blank Fretboard, Staff and Tab

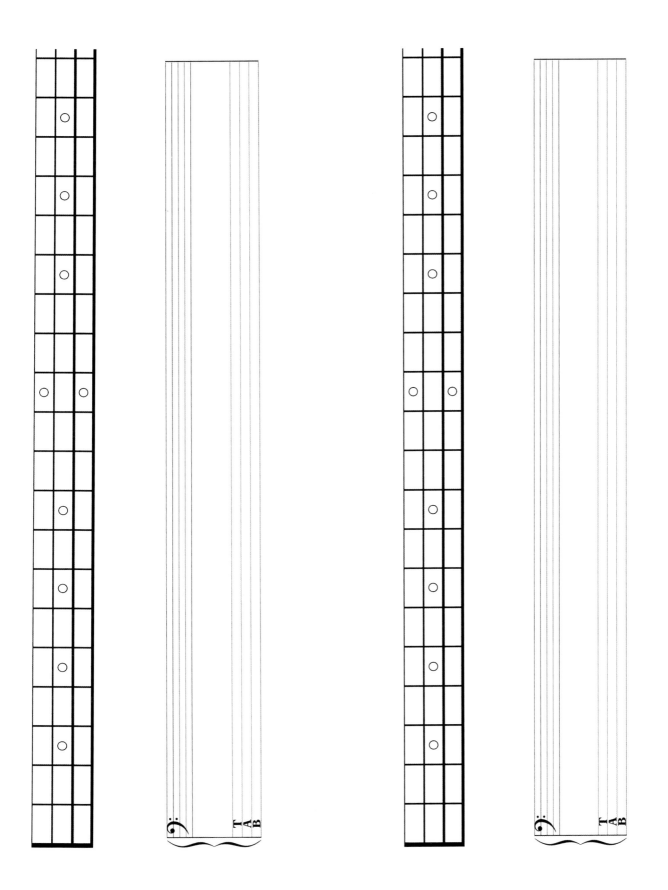

Print out and draw your *Scale Colour System* maps.

About The Author

A musician and educator, Alex Lofoco was born and raised in Rome, Italy. The strong passion for music developed in his early teens led him to embrace music as a performer, producer and educator.

He moved to London where he graduated in Popular Music Performance – BMus (Hons) at the University of West London. During his studies in London Alex started holding bass

photo by MusicOff.com

clinics and masterclasses, sharing his passion for research and innovation in music education with the students of the *Musicians Institute* (Los Angeles), the *BIMM Institute*, the *ICMP, Academies Of Music And Sound* (UK) and *Lizard Academies* (Italy).

Alex's debut album *Beyond* was released in December 2017 featuring an A-list of guest artists: keyboard wizard Jordan Rudess (Dream Theater), drummer Marco Minnemann (The Aristocrats, Steven Wilson), Eric Marienthal (Chick Corea Elektric Band), piano prodigy Jesús Molina and guitarist, composer and co-producer Roby Meola.

"Hugely impressive and incendiary debut album"
– The Progressive Aspect

Alex has been featured on numerous magazine and online communities such as *Bass Guitar Magazine, Bass Quarterly, Bajos Y Bajistas, Bass Musician Magazine, Chitarre, MusicOff.com, NoTreble.com.*

Alex is also a performing artist at international music shows such as the *Namm Show, Musikmesse, Euro Bass Day* and the *London Bass Guitar Show* amongst others.

Alex proudly endorses

www.alexlofoco.com